INFANTICIDE

AND THE HANDICAPPED NEWBORN

INFANTICIDE

AND THE HANDICAPPED NEWBORN

Edited by
Dennis J. Horan and Melinda Delahoyde

Brigham Young University Press

Library of Congress Cataloging in Publication Data

Main entry under title:

Infanticide and the handicapped newborn.

Includes bibliographical references and index.
1. Infanticide–United States–Moral and ethical aspects–Addresses, essays, lectures. 2. Euthanasia–United States–Moral and ethical aspects–Addresses, essays, lectures. 3. Infants (Newborn)–Legal status, laws, etc.–Addresses, essays, lectures. 4. Handicapped children–Law and legislation–United States–Addresses, essays, lectures. 5. Medical ethics–United States–Addresses, essays, lectures. I. Horan, Dennis J. II. Delahoyde, Melinda. [DNLM: 1. Infanticide. 2. Child, Exceptional abnormalities–Therapy. 3. Ethics, Medical. W 867 I428]
HV6541.U6I53   364.1'523   81-24203
ISBN 0-8425-2053-8

Brigham Young University Press, Provo, Utah 84602
© 1982 by Americans United for Life, Inc. All rights reserved
Printed in the United States of America

10 9 8 7 6 5 4 3 2 1

Contents

Acknowledgments

We gratefully acknowledge the work of Paige Cunningham, Edward Grant, Virginia Reuter, and Louise Kaegi without whom this book could not have been completed. We especially thank Patrick A. Trueman and Dr. Eugene F. Diamond for their great dedication to the success of the International Conference on Infanticide and the Handicapped Newborn, and to the publication of this book. Their outstanding efforts stand as a tribute to their commitment to the sanctity and dignity of all human life.

Introduction

Two outstanding American physicians had enormous influence on ethical standards in the practice of medicine in the third quarter of the twentieth century. One was Dr. Henry K. Beecher, anesthesiologist at Harvard Medical School. Beecher's 1959 article "Experimentation in Man"[1] reasoned with himself and his professional colleagues concerning the moral principles governing research with human subjects, and his 1966 landmark article "Ethics and Clinical Research"[2] analyzed twenty-two examples of unethical or questionable research. The examples were "not cited for the condemnation of individuals" (names were stricken from the reports), but for the correction of practice.

The other pioneer of the past quarter century was Dr. Leo Alexander, psychiatrist at Tufts Medical School, who drafted the *Nuremberg Code of Medical Ethics* used in the Nazi medical trials. From his interviews of the German doctors and his study of their barbarous experiments on "worthless" human beings, Dr. Alexander wrote his landmark 1949 article entitled "Medical Science under Dictatorship."[3]

We are now in another quarter century—the last, at least, in the twentieth century. And we have ample reason to ask whether the way we are is better than the way we were; whether the moral history of humankind has fallen further behind the scientific; whether, indeed, our sophistication in discussions of medical ethics and daily news reports of *this* breakthrough and *that* moral dilemma have not dulled our sensibility to some simple moral truths that Henry Beecher and Leo Alexander knew quite well.

Leo Alexander's statement that the Nazi medical crimes "started with small beginnings . . . with the acceptance of the attitude . . . that there is such a thing as a life not worthy to be lived" is well known and frequently quoted—for example, by Dr. Eugene F. Diamond and Dr. C. Everett Koop in the present volume. But Alexander tells us more than that concerning how such enormous crimes came to pass—or rather were brought about. A brief summary of Alexander's sociopolitical analysis should be a good introduction to the chapters that follow and will enable serious readers to put to themselves—and to our age—the question: In what manner or degree is there the same drift in the United States today and in Western societies generally?

"The German people," Alexander wrote, "were considered by their Nazi leaders more ready to accept the extermination of the sick than those for political reasons." That, so far, tells us that the Holocaust began with the incurably ill, who could no longer be of any social benefit and who indeed had to be maintained at social cost. But apparently the German people were not yet considered by their political leaders to be ready enough to accept the extermination of the incurably ill in general. Alexander tells us that to make dispatching such patients socially acceptable, the Nazis began with *defective children.*

So, there was inaugurated in Nazi Germany an organization devoted exclusively to the killing of children, known by the euphemistic name of "Realm's Committee for Scientific Approach to Severe Illness Due to Heredity and Constitution," and another organization, "The Charitable Transport Company for the Sick," to take them to their doom. The children were moved on conveyor belts, six to a furnace. The resulting mixed ashes were distributed to six urns and shipped to the families. Alexander comments that "this program was merely the entering wedge for exterminations of far greater scope in the *political* program of genocide of conquered nations and the *racially unwanted*" (my emphasis).

If I read his article correctly, the Holocaust began with "medically indicated" infanticide. This was among the "small beginnings" together with the first "small" shift in the attitudes of German doctors, which Leo Alexander generalized in the statement that is familiar to many people who do not know the context. "Whatever proportions these crimes finally assumed," he wrote, "it became evident to all who investigated them that *they started from small beginnings.* The beginnings at first were merely a subtle shift in emphasis in the basic attitude of the physicians. It started with the acceptance of the attitude . . . *that there is such a thing as a life not worthy to be lived*" (my emphasis). This attitude first embraced severely retarded children, then the chronically ill elderly, then politically and racially unwanted groups. "The impetus was the attitude toward the non-rehabilitable ill"—from infants who cannot be rehabilitated to social usefulness, to any patients who cannot, to classes of people in general who were not regarded as socially acceptable. Nazi Germans began first with unwanted defective infants, then lives not worth living in costly insane asylums, then the terminally ill, then Gypsies, homosexuals, et cetera; and having first bloodied themselves with killing their own kind, beginning with infants, came last of all to the Jews who as a group became the preponderance of the Holocaust.

The reader may be as amazed and incredulous as I was upon first reading Alexander's article that the way of entrance upon enormous crimes was across the fragile bodies and lives of small children. I have since lost my amazement. Consider signs of the drift today. In recent United States medical literature it has been proposed that it is somehow more acceptable to kill or neglect to death a poor-prognosis infant in the intensive care unit than an older terminal patient, because infants have no *apprehension* of what may be done to them. After all, any one of us may become aged, infirm, nonrehabilitable, or useless ballast; but no one reading these words will ever live long enough to become a child again. Apparently, one way to become a notable contemporary philosopher is to argue that children are not rights bearers; they have only conferred rights, bestowed upon them by rational contractors who are persons having shared projects and therefore rights, capable members of a society for which the children they choose to protect will qualify later. And if you are a scientist—anyway, a famous one—you can advocate that we should establish the practice of "delayed birth certificates" to select the future members of the human race. This idea will gain you some notoriety, but not likely any notable censure, moral opprobrium, or outrage even from those who disagree. By the test of what we are willing to discuss neutrally, as if any of several conclusions could be right in practice, we do not much respect small people.

Leo Alexander concluded his article by asking how sturdy were the ethics of the American medical profession. He asked whether "American physicians have also been infected with ... cold-blooded, utilitarian philosophy and whether early traces of it can be detected in their medical thinking that may make them vulnerable to departures of the type that occurred in Germany." By comparison with the Dutch physicians who resisted the very first step and measured by the standard of the Good Samaritan who "had no thought of nor did he actually care whether he could restore working capacity," Alexander was not very hopeful about American medicine. "Physicians have become dangerously close to being mere technicians of rehabilitation"; and "in an increasingly utilitarian society these patients [with chronic or incurable diseases] are being looked down upon with increasing definiteness as unwanted ballast." "Killing centers" were for him "a long but nevertheless logical step" from such an attitude. " 'What is useful is right' has infected society, including the medical portion."

Alexander seemed in the end to place more faith in intervening layers of organizations counteracting these trends. He mentions various citizen-patient and parents-of-patients voluntary groups concerned for the compassionate treatment of genetic defects, and research to discover therapies. These new societies, he says, have taken over "one of the ancient functions of medicine—namely, to give hope to the patient and to relieve his relatives."

Faced as he was by the political and moral "reeducation" of the medical profession and the German people by their political leaders, it is understandable that Alexander placed his trust in "voluntary associations" that stand between the individual and *the state*. Rereading his article on Nazi medical practices, I could not fail to be reminded of the fact that many of the patient-oriented associations he hoped would save us from a utilitarian medical practice and public policy have themselves switched over to "thinking in terms of destructive rather than ameliorative terms."

The chapters that follow were papers presented at the International Conference on Infanticide and the Handicapped Newborn, held in Chicago at the O'Hare Hilton Hotel, December 6, 1980. A conference on infanticide? Anyone who knows something about the reckless rush to deliberate infanticide in the last decade will say, "It's about time!" Sponsored by Americans United for Life? Some will say, "Oh, that's one of those 'special interest' groups!" Those who respond in this way identify themselves as part of the problem, as people content to live in the twilight of Western civilization, undisturbed by the technological Holocaust that has broken out in all the "developed," industrialized countries. Some things were better done with passion, loathing, and hatred than with "compassion" and with a manufacturing efficiency that "selects" the "products" to be saved and makes all of them obsolescent.

There are, however, major disagreements among the authors. Some believe that infants born with defects incompatible with life need (and deserve) to be given extraordinary care and treatments. Some believe that they should be given the same care as normal "preemies"; this suggests a larger role for physician discretion while his actions are still rule-governed. Some may widen that discretion by resort to "substantial judgments," case by case, based on objective determination of the specific interests of the patient. These disagreements are in the main implicit; and I am not sure what, if they are important, they amount to.

Some argue or assume that infanticide logically and causally has followed from the widespread practice of legalized, elective abortion, and has been a further corruption of medicine's mission, a corruption that was foreseeable at the outset. Others do not assume this to be true and, without explicitly arguing the point, concentrate attention on one or another specific approach to infanticide. One can say that this is a book about infanticide, *with* or *without* the abortion toboggan. It can be read with profit—and it is to be hoped with awakened moral indignation—by anyone who disagrees with some of the authors either about the morality of abortion or about the connection between abortion and infanticide.

There is also a commendable variety and multiplicity in the approaches the authors take to their common topic. Victor G. Rosenblum and Michael L. Budde consider infanticide as practiced in times past and by other societies, and recent interpretations of the phenomenon. This provides needed historical perspective. Rosenblum also makes observations, in broad terms, on the social and cultural environment of the defective child. Three authors, Dennis J. Horan, Steven R. Valentine, and John A. Robertson, discuss the law of homicide and agree that the announced practice of neglecting to save defective infants is clearly criminal—and that the *practice* should give way, not the law. Informative medical chapters are those by Dr. Craig L. Anderson on modern achievements in premature infant salvage and by Drs. James T. Brown and David G. McLone on treatment choices for infants with meningomyelocele. These are the most purely objective reports of all the contributions. Other chapters are instructive on medical and other aspects of which readers need to be aware—those by Drs. Eugene F. Diamond and C. Everett Koop, for example. Drs. Diamond and Koop also, quite properly, engage in ethical reasoning and moral advocacy. The one professional ethicist among the participants, Arthur J. Dyck, has written a splendid chapter.

I have left to the last mention of the chapter by Jérôme LeJeune. His is also a purely informative chapter, but its special importance is that his topic is the prospect of developing therapies that can correct deficiencies in intelligence in preborn children *in utero*. I do not pretend to understand Dr. LeJeune's learned chapter completely, but I can comprehend enough to justify further comment on what appears to be the crucial import of his message.

We read recently the news of an exquisite procedure by which a medical team inserted a "needle" transabdominably into a woman's uterus to kill a defective *twin* so that the normal one alone could be brought to birth. I would say that accomplishment was an improvement over what is now done in the case of male twins of women who are carriers of the gene for hemophilia: *both* preborns are now aborted, and that destroys a normal male in *half* the times. So I fail to understand the special stirring of negative emotions over the *skilled* destruction of one *afflicted* twin. If you are willing to assume that the treatment of choice for an affliction is the destruction of the one who suffers the affliction, then that is *technically* admirable.

The foregoing is background for a sober reflection on the various exquisite *therapies* LeJeune sees on the horizon, or at least as possible future medical procedure. How can new therapies for the cure of handicapped infants be developed unless the practice of letting salvageable handicapped infants die, even hastening their deaths, is stopped? Infanticide and the discovery of therapies to save and care for infants pull in opposite directions. A familiar principle governing the morality of *trial treatments* is that the possible benefit brings with it no risk of greater harm to the patient than the defect he now suffers and for which a cure is sought. This means that there are therapies that cannot ethically be developed by experimentally treating children who suffer only some mild degree of the defect in question. Whether this is true of the particular therapies LeJeune discusses I do not know; but it is commonly assumed that any new trial treatment brings with it an unknown incidence of risk of unknown harm.

And finally, what of that endangered species—physicians like Jérôme LeJeune who are entirely devoted to care and treatment—if neonatal infanticide becomes standard medical practice for the "prevention" of serious defects in children?

Above, I called attention to the fact that some of the contributors implicitly disagree with others on the question of the morality of abortion and/or on the connection of abortion with infanticide. At least, some do not address these questions; others do. The common target of each chapter is the policy or practice of negligent or active infanticide of defective children. I drew attention to this disagreement or disregard of those questions in order to urge that this volume of essays be read by persons who may not have thought of such a connection or who may disagree with a (probable) majority of the contributors on the morality of abortion.

We need to restore the already shattered consensus that our law, the medical profession, nurses, parents—indeed, strangers—have a positive obligation to protect, and should *never* neglect, whatever be their benign motives, individual human beings who have been born into the human community. If the absolute right of privacy to control one's own reproductive life does not run into an absolute limit *here,* then there are no indefeasible claims of any others upon us that cannot be thought and discussed *away.*

Before concluding this introduction, I should state briefly my own views on the morality of elective abortion and the connection of that practice with the practice of infanticide. Candor requires this of me, but without withdrawing my insistence that this volume can and should be read by people who disagree on these questions.

*   *   *

On January 24, 1973, two days after *Roe v. Wade* and *Doe v. Bolton,* I wrote the following letter to the *New York Times.*[4]

To the Editor:

Speaking for the majority in the Supreme Court's abortion decision, Justice Blackmun spoke of a viable baby as only a "potential" life. Also, concerning the remnant of legislative authority graciously left to the people and their representatives, he wrote in only a hypothetical vein: "*If* the state is interested in protecting fetal life after viability. . . ." If? Furthermore, he described the grounds for compelling state interest in the unborn as their "capability of meaningful life outside the mother's womb." Meaningful? Thus the Court opened the door to weighing human lives according to comparative worthiness, or something called "meaningfulness."

Ineluctably we pass from abortion to infanticide, whether the justices know it or not. Ineluctably, because many of the reasons alleged to justify permissive abortion have equal force in justifying the killing of neonates in hospital nurseries.

Long ago, from studying polls of public opinion in this country, the pro-abortion people decided that the only way to success for their cause was through the courts. Whoever is concerned about one-man rule in the Presidency, to the erosion of Congressional authority, ought to be equally worried about seven-man rule in the judiciary, gathering to itself the legislative power on important public questions that formerly belonged to the people and their elected representatives to decide.

Princeton University   Paul Ramsey
Jan. 24, 1973

This letter was published on Saturday, February 3.

That weekend I was at a meeting at the Hastings Center-Institute of Society, Ethics and the Life Sciences. On Saturday night there was a party for all the participants at the home of Daniel and Sidney Callahan. During the course of the evening, a wife of one of the younger staff of the Hastings Center confronted me; I say confronted not because of any unpleasantness but because of the evident restrained moral passion with which she spoke about my statement, "Ineluctably we pass from abortion to infanticide, whether the justices know it or not." If you are right, she said, then we ought to *accept infanticide* rather than impose legal limitations on the freedom of abortion. This being a social occasion, I shrugged and mumbled something about that being an opinion I obviously did not share.

Looking back, I think I wanted to terminate that conversation also because of my shock at what had just been said. In the summer of 1970 I had published an article, entitled "Feticide/Infanticide Upon Request,"⁵ that I believed was not only logically compelling but also a persuasive argument against the draft of a United Methodist Church paper on abortion. Later that same year my most sustained analysis of the morality of abortion appeared in a chapter entitled "Some Reference Points in Deciding about Abortion," in John T. Noonan's *The Morality of Abortion.*⁶ I endeavored in that chapter simply to set forth an agenda for reasonable discourse concerning the question. I proposed two overlapping criteria for distinguishing a good from a bad argument for permissive abortion practice: first, a good argument should not avoid giving *some* reasonable answer to the crucial question, When does an individuated human life begin?; and second, a good argument for abortion must not at the same time be an argument for infanticide.

Pointing out the connection between some of the justifications for some abortion practices and most of the alleged justifications for the practice of infanticide was already, when put forward, a failed argument—one that failed *to persuade.* Indeed, the startling fact was that the argument not only failed to persuade, it was counterproductive. To link in any way the idea of abortion with the idea of infanticide, I soon discovered, was to promote the acceptability of the latter in hitherto innocent minds.

Of course, a rationally compelling argument can fail to be persuasive, and a proposed test for telling the difference between a good and a bad argument for permissive abortion can be correct while it still influences some people morally to accept the associated evil (in this instance, infanticide). Nevertheless, the effects were puzzling. Why did the influences run in a different direction from that stated by the argument?

Can my puzzlement be explicated? Yes, but the explanation is paradoxical. *The arguments failed precisely because they were and are true.* The characterization of infanticide as similar in significant moral respects to abortion-by-choice must necessarily fail to persuade any individual, or society, that is already deeply committed to the right of elective abortion. The more firmly the connection is established, the more people who endorse elective abortion may be impelled to accept the practice of infanticide. Thus, our society had suddenly become, or rather it had manifested itself to be, both pro-abortion and infanticidal. Given these conditions, the "entering edge of the wedge" argument (which is a good *argument*) may fail to persuade or may even prove to be counterproductive (if the connection affirmed by the argument is demonstrated convincingly enough and is believed unbreakable). The more the argument works as a reason, the less it may work as a persuader.

Above all, the wedge argument must not be dismissed on a superficial understanding of it. It does not mean—never has meant—a mere prediction that if we do X we will cause ourselves to do Y, and since Y is wrong we should not start the sequence by doing X. The prediction is based on the *internal reasons* justifying one kind of action and then equally another kind of action, and not on one action causing another. Thus, when I affirmed in my letter to the *Times* that ineluctably we pass from abortion to infanticide, my next words were: "Ineluctably, *because many of the reasons* alleged to justify permissive abortion *have equal force* in justifying the killing of neonates in hospital nurseries" (emphasis added). The argument does not say that, because of some sort of physical or social necessity, we *cannot* stop at one or more points down the slippery slope. It says, rather, that, where there are no overriding counterreasons for not doing Y for the same reasons we invoked to justify doing X, there are no sufficient good reasons for stopping. There is always some principle, some consistency in moral judgments, some coherence of moral reasons concerning similar cases, behind hammering the wedge in deeper, or inviting us to do the same kind of thing further down the slope.[7]

Sentimental souls believe—or sometimes say they believe—that we can draw a line on the continuum of human life at *birth,* or *viability,* or detection of *brain waves,* et cetera. After one or another line has been passed in human development, they say, there is an equal congener among us, a human being as inviolate as is any other human being from assault or wrongful death. In the *theoretical* order, such like assertions can be disputed forever. In the *practical* order, however, nothing can be clearer than *there is no such line.*

Genetic abortion and genetic infanticide are equivalents. Social, economic, or familial indices for abortion are the same indices used in the announced practice of negligent infanticide. The prevention of lives suffering mental and physical defect serious to "x" degree by eliminating those lives applies to preborns and to infants alike, since the "good reason" applies to both. Abortion for the sake of the fetus is only renamed "the wrong or injury of continued existence." So also the terms used to put what we are doing in a different category than the reality. So "product of conception" was once a reference to a seriously defective preborn; it is used more and more of infants. The force of all such reasons and terminological disguises skips easily across lines like brain waves, viability, and birth. Nothing makes this plainer than the fact that there needed to be a *conference* on the increasing tolerance of the practice of infanticide in our society–"birth," et cetera, to the contrary notwithstanding.

I devoutly hope I am mistaken in this. But I think I am not. However, I repeat, this time as an advocate: this is a book about infanticide, *with* or *without* the abortion toboggan. Any boundaries that can be fixed or preserved today are precious, and should be cherished and strengthened–however nonrational they may be. So if readers of this volume disagree with some or most of the authors either on the morality of abortion or the connection of the practice of infanticide with our current practice of abortion, and if they join with these and other of their fellow physicians, nurses, lawyers, clergymen, and fellow citizens generally in an alert and informed movement to hold the line against dealing death to infants, and stopping the practice of selective neglect: that will be all to the good.

For me to invite this with conviction is only another reading of the "entering edge of the wedge" argument. For the sanctity of human life is what I may call a *global* moral outlook. Whoever strengthens the protectability of life on one side of any line distinguishing human beings from one another in this respect, strengthens it also on the other. If many of the reasons alleged to justify permissive abortion have equal force in justifying hastening the deaths of neonates, it is equally true that many of the reasons alleged to justify the announced practice of infanticide have equal force (and are needed) to justify elective abortion. Therefore the so-called "pro-life" movement logically simply cannot be single-issue advocacy; nor can opposition to infanticide fail to be "pro-life." These are only bands on the spectrum of a human life span. One band or another may be the focus of one person's or group's intellectual attention, and the focus also of their moral outrage over violated sanctity. Still, the sanctity of human life is one and indivisible.

What Leo Alexander called a "cold-blooded, utilitarian philosophy" is also a *global* moral outlook–one that devours all her children, whatever their size or age or dependence. Against an increasingly utilitarian society, and similar bureaucratic policy thinking in the professions and the intervening associations in which Alexander rested his hope, there is no line to be drawn and no limit that can be set. The requiredness of *the equality of life* and calculating or weighing *the quality of life* in measuring out our care and protection are moral outlooks irrepressibly in conflict. In such a cause, this volume is quite properly a call to partisans who choose life.

Paul Ramsey

Department of Religion
Princeton University

Notes

1. Beecher, *Experimentation in Man,* 169 J.A.M.A. 461 (1959).

2. *Id.; Ethics and Clinical Research,* 274 NEW ENGLAND J. MED. 1354 (1966).

3. Alexander, *Medical Science Under Dictatorship,* 241 NEW ENGLAND J. MED. 39 (1949).

4. Earlier that month, on January 10, speaking at the annual legislative banquet of the Minnesota Citizens Concerned for Life, in the Twin Cities, I predicted the way of privacy the Supreme Court's decision would go. Marjorie Mecklenburg did a tremendous job smoothing ruffled feathers during the reception afterward—over me, an outsider, coming in and speaking against the moral ethos of that state nourished so well by the Lutherans, Catholics, and others in MCCL! She told me since, with characteristic good humor, that I prepared them for the shock over what twelve days later the Supreme Court took away from them.

5. Ramsey, *Feticide/Infanticide Upon Request,* 39 RELIGION IN LIFE 170 (1970), *reprinted in* THREE ON ABORTION (Child and Family Reprint Series), at 63 (1978).

6. Ramsey, *Some Reference Points in Deciding About Abortion,* in THE MORALITY OF ABORTION: LEGAL AND HISTORICAL PERSPECTIVES 60 (J. Noonan, Jr. ed. 1970).

7. *See* Ramsey, *The Wedge: Not So Simple,* 3 HASTINGS CENTER REP. 11–12 (1971).

1
Historical and Cultural Considerations of Infanticide

Victor G. Rosenblum and Michael L. Budde

Judging from the relevant literature, the practice of infanticide has not been limited to any one time, place, or cultural climate. Indeed, while drawing upon various justifications for the practice, almost all cultures have had at least some experience with more than merely "isolated incidents" of infanticide.

The sweep of infanticidal practice has been broad, ranging from primitive hunter-gatherer societies to the most advanced. That Western civilizations of recent vintage have had considerable experience with infanticide may surprise some; yet, to buttress such a claim, one need only refer to one expert who concludes that infanticide accounted for approximately 6 percent of all violent deaths in England as late as 1878,[1] while another characterized France of a century earlier as engaged in an "all-out war against infants."[2]

Of the several reasons that have been advanced to explain the practice of infanticide, seven are primary: family planning, reduction of the female population, avoidance of social stigma (particularly that of illegitimacy), economic incentive, elimination of handicapped offspring, ritual sacrifice, and superstitions.

Most of these justifications were more or less bound to specific cultural environments, but a few of them—particularly the elimination of handicapped offspring—ran through almost all infanticidal cultures. When several have been present simultaneously in a given setting, as was the case in medieval Europe, their impact has been considerable. Infanticide was thought to be the most frequently committed crime in all of Europe up to 1800.[3]

Victor G. Rosenblum received his B.A. and J.D. from Columbia University, and his Ph.D. from the University of California, Berkeley. He is currently Professor of Law and Political Science, Northwestern University. He is Past President of Reed College.

Michael L. Budde received his B.A. from Northwestern University School of Journalism. He is currently Director of Legislative Affairs for the Michigan Citizens for Life.

Among the major factors contributing to the epidemic of infanticide during that period, the stigma associated with illegitimacy was among the most powerful. A brief examination will reveal how social forces tend to precipitate, if not promote, infanticide in a given cultural setting.

In many cultures in which illegitimate birth brought scorn and rejection upon the unwed mother, infanticide was a frequent recourse. Such was indeed the case in western Europe, where both church and state dealt severely with an unmarried mother and her child, to such a degree that some historians have left the blame for infanticide during the period on the doorstep of the church.[4]

At a church synod in England in 787–88, for example, the right to inherit property was withdrawn from illegitimate children, a move followed thereafter by a refusal of state and church to accept bastard children as citizens or communicants.[5] These sanctions continued for centuries, with others added subsequently.

Unwed mothers were also subject to considerable degradation. Church officials often forced unwed mothers through a humiliating public penance service, which involved systematic torment and abuse from the lay membership as well as the clergy. Of this penance requirement, Oskar Helmuth Werner, a major source of scholarship on the era, writes:

> Undoubtedly, many a poor girl yielded to this requirement because she believed, as she had been taught, that only those who were in the fold of the church could reach heaven, while many others attempted to remain chaste in the eyes of the church by concealing her (pregnant) condition and then killing her child.[6]

Professor Selwyn Smith, in his historical overview of the maltreatment of children, provides a glimpse at the lot of the handicapped child at various stages in history.

> Twins, monstrous births, or congenitally defective children were feared by men as they frequently foreshadowed evils. In China, India and throughout the Orient, deformed children were usually destroyed at birth. The Greeks and Romans killed their weak and deformed infants in the superstitious hope that only the strong would survive. Plato, Aristotle and other philosophers lectured that survival of the fittest was necessary to strengthen the race and this belief was incorporated into the Roman law of the Twelve Tables which forbade rearing deformed children. During the period of the Caesars, infanticide—always legal in Rome—received the approval of philosophers like Seneca.[7]

Oskar Werner further describes infanticide in the Roman context.

It was the suffering which the imperfectability of the child entailed upon itself and its fellows that caused its elimination from the human family. . . . The father was permitted under certain circumstances to put to death children under three years of age if they had been declared monstrous by five neighbors.[8]

Perhaps the most telling statement comes from anthropologist Laila Williamson, who concludes that

[i]nfanticide may be widespread in a society or happen only occasionally, but it has very few, if any, exceptions with one class of infants, that is, deformed infants. The reasons for eugenic infanticide seem obvious: unwillingness or inability to assume the burden for caring for such an infant, whose future at best would be unsure. The same is true of infants who are clearly "different," as, for instance, those with unusual skin color, too light or too dark.[9]

The *pro forma* respect for life that has been important in many cultures shows its limits in consideration of the disabled. An important consideration is the process of relegating infants, particularly the disabled, to a less-than-human status. While this dehumanization, or "pseudo-speciation" as others have called it,[10] has applied to all newborns at various times, it has traditionally applied with uncommon force to the disabled child.

Writing about the infanticidal mothers whose children frequently found final rest in the sewers of medieval Paris, Professor Maria Piers notes: "We can further surmise that they (the mothers) were unfeeling toward the children they had borne. The babies must have appeared to them as strange things—not as fellow human beings or as helpless creatures—but as waste, as near inanimate objects that were perhaps despicable."[11]

In another context, Piers observes that "neglect reduces a small child in a short time to an unresponsive, totally passive creature who soon appears subhuman, almost vegetable like. Dehumanization of the doomed child was a technique, albeit often an unconscious one, that parents followed on and off throughout history."[12]

Echoing this theme, William Langer, in his historical examination of infanticide and population control, explains the phenomenon in part by noting that "the newborn bear little resemblance to more mature human beings or even to year-old children. Strong maternal feelings evidently are aroused only on the second or third day after giving birth, when nursing begins. Thus it is not surprising that among so many people at so many different times in history the disposal of unwanted babies has been accepted as a matter of course.[13]

Also important to an understanding of dehumanizing influences is attention to the role and status of children. In varying degrees, children have not been accorded the status of equal, independent actors in society; their identity has been closely linked with that of their family, and to the desires of their parents. Again, Werner makes this point clearly.

> People naively looked upon the child as the fruit and property of parents and found in abortion, exposure and infanticide nothing sinful. The moral duty to the newborn child was a development of a later civilization.[14]

Crucial to an understanding of infanticide in its social and cultural surroundings is some sense of how cultures adapt and/or contribute to infanticidal practices in their midst.

Widespread infanticide in many societies, particularly those of Judeo-Christian heritage, posed serious contradictions between social arrangements that protected human life on one hand and encouraged infanticide on the other. In western Europe, for example, conflicting social forces interacted to provide a curious double standard in which infanticide committed by the child's mother was a capital offense, while the same crime committed by another, generally a wet nurse or midwife, generally went unpunished.[15] Among the most common predicates of an infanticidal act during the Middle Ages and beyond was the "farming out" of babies to wet nurses, many of whom nursed several children simultaneously. The death rate for children sent to baby farms was high. Many such children were reported to have succumbed as a result of smothering ("overlaying") caused by the wet nurse rolling atop the child while it slept. This apparent accident was generally understood to be no accident at all, but nevertheless went unpunished. William Langer notes that

> Women in factory towns, working outside the home and in no position to care for a child, entrusted their infants to hired nurses—baby farmers who usually cared for their charges by putting them to sleep with narcotics. Many of them never reawakened.[16]

Eventually, infanticide created within European society "a complex of defense mechanisms that protected the community or certain elements of it from feeling guilty. At the same time it afforded them a way to get rid of unwanted children. The complex differed somewhat in time and place, depending on economic factors, on population statistics, and on prevailing lifestyles."[17]

Among the most common of the defense mechanisms utilized was a process of projection, whereby outcasts were blamed for the detested, yet implicitly condoned, deeds.

In describing this phenomenon, Piers notes:

> Those in power created outcastes such as wet nurses or those in foundling homes to do the killing, and another group, usually the

helpless mothers, to die for the sin of killing and thereby redeeming everybody else. . . . It was, for instance, known that the Chinese killed infants. But they were considered heathens. Other 'bad' people also killed children; the trash that wandered into the cities, or before that, it was the Jews or witches who did such ghastly things to babies. But never, ever one's own kind. For this 'fact,' the rich and powerful could and did profusely thank God.[18]

Eventually, however, the contradictions became too intense and the mechanisms began to break down. In nations across Europe, reform movements began to take shape, pressing for social and political changes that would eliminate infanticide. In Germany, for example, the prestigious Mannheim Theater sponsored an essay contest in the 1780s on the problem of infanticide. Approximately 400 essays were submitted.[19]

Of the early German reform movement, Werner observes:

The assertion that the literature on the subject [of infanticide] came entirely from the camp of the "philanthropists" is untenable, for infanticide was of interest to every school of thought and to men of every profession, to old and young, to the learned and unlearned. . . . It is important to remember that the discussion of infanticide was not limited to a few "stormy" youths . . . but that sagacious men of every calling devoted a part of their best efforts to an intent to solve this problem.[20]

While a ruler like Frederick the Great took a deep and personal interest in the problem of infanticide, such compassion was difficult to find among others of the privileged classes. Piers remarks that "on the whole, the powerful and respectable did not join the ranks of the reformers because they were unable to admit to the lethal discrimination against women—particularly poor women—and their unwanted children. Had they done so, they would have been overwhelmed by guilt feelings."[21]

Change finally did come, after centuries of laissez-faire infanticide, and as a result of concerted efforts of many individuals who championed reform. One such champion was Dr. William Burke Ryan, whose essay "Infanticide and its Medico-Legal Relations" won a gold medal in an English essay contest in the 1860s. Ryan urged his fellows to greater care for the unwed mother, asking:

Let society, if possible, look on the fact of illegitimate pregnancy with a more forgiving eye, and pity, at all events, the unhappy victims of seduction or the otherwise innocent who may have fallen. Let such victims have their future course through life of a less hopeless character; let them feel that an occasional flower may be scattered on the thorny path that lies before them, and that a green spot may now and then glad their eyes and give rest to their limbs; that life is not to be so wholly unendurable a character as they may suppose.[22]

Unwed mothers were eventually given most of the rights of married women, and, as Werner notes, "The attitude toward the fallen girl was changing from one of utter abhorrence to one of pity, even if this pity did not always express itself in acts. Maternity houses and homes of refuge for the unmarried mother were established everywhere in Europe. The illegitimate child was accepted into the community of church and state, and into trades and unions, after it had been barred from such privileges for centuries."[23]

In England many organizations labored to put an end to infanticide during the 1860s and 1870s. One of these, the Infant Life Protection Society, persuaded Parliament in 1872 to pass an act requiring that baby farms be specially licensed, and that such farms maintain full records of admissions and mortality, thus discouraging infanticide.[24] Another British organization, the Harveian Society's Committee on Infanticide, recommended in 1867 several social reforms, among them:

improved social support for destitute women;

regulation of wet nurses and an ending of baby-farm abuses;

the prohibition of infants or young children being the subject of life insurance policies (a frequent practice of the time that provided considerable economic incentive to commit infanticide);

increased governmental attention to the causes of illegitimacy and infanticide; and

legal reforms relating to the definition of birth and punishment for infanticide (both of which hindered effective prosecution of the crime).[25]

Infanticide as presently practiced and proposed is discussed elsewhere in this volume and in other sources.[26] It seems appropriate, however, after examining some of the history of infanticide, to consider the relationship of contemporary infanticide to its historical antecedents. A more complete understanding of contemporary infanticide can be gleaned from understanding both the similarities and dissimilarities to general historical patterns and practices.

This section focuses on two important themes common to contemporary infanticide and its practice in other times and cultures, namely the status of, and attitudes toward, the disabled; and the development of social patterns that tolerate or in some way encourage infanticide while still attempting to preserve a commitment to protection of all human beings.

Historically, the lot of handicapped children has generally not been happy (as discussed previously in this chapter). The objects of superstition, fear, and hostility, children with physical and mental deficiencies have been weeded out by infanticide for millennia. In cultures engaging in eugenic infanticide, such children have been considered, explicitly or implicitly, as being of only marginal value. And, while prevailing social myths change, the basic rationale behind eugenic infanticide remains remarkably stable and unchanging—the disabled are inferior—or they are threatening—and ought to be weeded out.

The status of the disabled is better in modern times than in times past, but not overwhelmingly so. Dr. R. William English thinks that "nearly half of the nondisabled public have primarily negative attitudes toward physically disabled persons."[27] There is also evidence indicating that men as a group and parents in lower economic and social brackets tend to be less accepting of the handicapped.[28]

Regarding the contemporary American society, Professor Leo Buscaglia is of the opinion that "though they may not be aware of it at the time, the infant born with a birth defect ... will be limited in not so much as the actual disability as much as by society's attitude regarding the disability. It is society, for the most part, that will define the disability of the handicapped and it is the individual who will suffer from that definition."[29]

Certain sectors of society, according to some evidence, have attitudes less tolerant of the handicapped because of an excessive focus on the disability rather than on the entire person. Perhaps most important are members of the medical profession, whose views continue to play a major role in contemporary debates on infanticide. Dr. English observes that

> certain types of contact between the non-disabled and the disabled may actually result in the development of more negative attitudes (stigma) on the part of the non-disabled. Research has shown that some hospital and medical workers develop more negative attitudes toward the physically disabled over time. This finding might be explained by the fact that interaction between the non-disabled and the disabled in a hospital setting tends to be generally superficial and involves individuals of unequal status position. Furthermore, hospitalization implies that the disabled person is placed in a dependent position, where materially he contributes less to the non-disabled than that person does to him. Such a situation could create resentment and hostility toward the disabled.[30]

Commenting on her study of mothers of children born with thalidomide-induced birth defects, Ethel Roskies notes that "the perspective of the mother may be very different from the perspective of researchers and clinicians in the area. Professionals become involved with deviant children because they are different, and the usual emphasis is on the extent of the difference."[31] The mothers who were able to accept their children, Roskies concludes, were able to do so because they could see beyond the multiple differences and accept their child as a human being first and handicapped only secondarily.[32]

It is obvious that negative attitudes toward the disabled, whatever their source, have influenced the infanticide debate in recent years. For example, an interim report by a task force of the Anglican Church of Canada in 1977 refers to disabled newborns as "human-looking shapes," or at best "sentient" creatures: ". . . the only way to treat such defective infants humanely is not to treat them as human."[33] Another example is the effect of language as indicators and in turn shapers of attitudes toward the disabled. Popularly, the infanticide debate includes terms like "vegetables," "monsters," and some even less endearing. One commentator outlines the deleterious effects of such pejorative terminology, particularly that used by medical personnel to the parents of a handicapped child. "When the doctor describes her baby in terms usually reserved for foreigners or monkeys, it is not surprising that the mother will hesitate to welcome it into her home."[34]

This process of dehumanization is closely related to hostility toward the disabled. Historically, it seems reasonable to suggest that frequently, without such a process, infanticide could not take root or exist in a society without provoking considerable social backlash. Dehumanization has been a near constant in past experiences with infanticide, and its currency is evident in the still-tenacious notion that children are the "property" of their parents (and hence expendable at their request), and in legal proposals that seek to remove the protection associated with "personhood" from newborns judged to be substandard.

No society that professes a *pro forma* dedication to the inviolability of innocent lives can develop a system of infanticide without making significant social adjustments. This surely has been the case historically in western Europe. Therefore, the important and frequently contradictory developments regarding infanticide as proposed and practiced in the United States should come as no surprise.

Ironically, advocacy of infanticide comes at a time when the rights and respectability of disabled persons are expanding significantly. Called the "last minority" by one writer,[35] the handicapped have been the instigators (and beneficiaries) of increased legal and social sensitivity to the role of the disabled in society. A French-sponsored United Nations declaration in 1971, for example, proclaimed that "The mentally retarded person has to the maximum degree of feasibility the same rights as other human beings,"[36] while the decade of the 1970s generally saw greater emphasis on civil rights legislation as a vehicle for the advancement of the interests of disabled persons.[37]

Much has also been accomplished in increasing the sensitivity of the general public to the barriers constructed—consciously and unconsciously—that prevent the disabled from existing as persons of social status equal to "normal" persons. One leader in this drive, Professor Jacobus TenBroek, denounces what he calls "attitudes which not infrequently are quite erroneous and misconceived" that limit the disabled. Such attitudes, in his opinion, involve everything from misplaced concerns about safety and protection to, perhaps more significantly, "public aversion to the sight of them (the disabled) and the conspicuous reminder of their plight."[38]

It might at first glance seem curious, then, that the issue of infanticide has received such a favorable hearing in a climate so receptive to improving the social status of the disabled. That the two can develop side by side, frequently involving members of the same professional classes, leads to the following observations and speculations.

First, it seems reasonable to wonder whether the increasing toleration for infanticide will not in fact damage the efforts of those seeking to improve life for the disabled. Professor Robert Burt puts the issue squarely on the table when he observes:

> In recent years, those working with the mentally retarded have documented the destructive inappropriateness of institutional placement for most children consigned there. . . . All seem agreed, at least in principle, that the proper remedy is to insist on community life for retarded children, to press every effort toward keeping such children living with their families and to provide the families with extensive community support toward realizing the fullest potential for these children.

> Proposals to authorize withholding treatment from defective newborns cut against the force of social commitment to this course. If there is a socially sanctioned mechanism for ending the lives of deformed infants—whether that sanction extends to the parents and physicians alone or requires some external approval of their decision—the question will be insistently posed for every obviously deformed child and his parents: why was this child permitted to live?[39]

Why indeed? The impetus to institute massive, expensive, and potentially difficult programs to mainstream the disabled seems threatened by a concurrent policy that places virtually no value on such persons at birth. The issue is far from merely an academic exercise. How it is resolved promises to affect not only the disabled in the neonatal period, but the status of disabled persons generally. The private decisions of parents and physicians regarding their children will doubtless have important public consequences.

It seems equally appropriate to inquire whether, in at least an attenuated fashion, our increased efforts to improve the status of the disabled has in fact made infanticide an *easier* idea with which to live. Professor Piers and others have detailed the complex social double standards that have made infanticidal systems possible in other times—efforts that on one hand assuaged the public sense of compassion and respect for persons, and on the other hand allowed them to weed out the undesirable without an accompanying sense of guilt. It may be argued that such is recurring in today's society. With so much emphasis on improved neonatal care, with the disabled becoming more accepted as full members of society, how can anyone charge that we are insensitive to the plight of disabled newborns? As long as the infanticidal processes move discreetly, allowing public pretense to exist relatively unaffected, a kind of balance can be struck between fulfilling our obligations to the less fortunate and eliminating them when such is politically feasible and not overly threatening or embarrassing. Attorney F. Raymond Marks, a participant in a prestigious conference on infanticide, stated the issue most directly.

> We now "let go" of some babies notwithstanding the rules against euthanasia. . . . But we do not announce this to the world. Such practice allows the actors to hide from themselves the fact that they have changed or departed from the rule while announcing their strict adherence to the absolute rule of sanctity of life in all cases.[40]

A curious double standard has long existed regarding efforts to improve the status of the disabled. Although some interest has been generated by speeches, platitudes, and solemn commitments, substantially less has been produced in terms of actual results. Current attempts to gain greater acceptance of the disabled are not proceeding without resistance—for example, community opposition to "mainstreaming," or involving the mentally or physically impaired in local living situations when feasible—has been met with considerable opposition in some areas.[41] Another example is budget cuts made by some governmental agencies; in many instances the most severe cutbacks have been forced upon programs for the disabled. Into this drama enters the disabled newborn, a new actor (in terms of policy) in an old setting.

The contemporary situation regarding infanticide is apparently not unique; it seems that every aspect has a general historical antecedent. Yet, three wrinkles in the contemporary situation deserve at least brief mention, for they may, upon more extensive investigation than is possible here, reveal considerations or perspectives that can be useful in reaching a more complete understanding of neonatal euthanasia in Western cultures.

Many historians contend that where abortion has been dangerous or inaccessible, infanticide has been found to occur with greater frequency. Similarly, as the number of abortions increases, the incidence of infanticide decreases. This body of scholarship, however, generally concentrates on eras when selective abortion to eliminate defective offspring had not been developed; hence, the motivations for abortion were for other than eugenic reasons.

In our day, the emergence of abortion that is readily available for any reason, including use in concert with eugenic prenatal screening programs, has not reduced the incidence or enthusiasm for eugenic infanticide. Quite the opposite. The paradox of our era is that, although the number of abortions has climbed into the millions, including thousands for eugenic reasons alone, infanticide may not be decreasing at all. It may in fact be increasing. Such a determination is problematic, however, given the lack of reliable statistical information concerning the incidence of infanticide both before and after *Roe v. Wade*. Nevertheless, it appears that the classic relationship of increased abortions with decreased infanticide may not apply in the present situation. Rather, in addition to providing greater social acceptability for infanticide, abortion may be a contributing factor to an increase in infanticide.

Although findings are as yet tentative, one researcher has indicated a possible link between the legitimization of abortion and the increased incidence of child abuse. Writing in the *Canadian Journal of Psychiatry*, Professor Philip Ney maintains that, by transgressing traditional taboos against violence toward children, abortion may actually increase the occurrence of child abuse.[42] It seems plausible that, if such a relationship (however tenuous) exists on a societal level, it may well apply to an increased tolerance for infanticide. Whether such is in fact the case remains to be seen, but given the similarities in the controlling premises of abortion, child abuse, and infanticide (the child as property of parents rather than an inviolable entity, for example), further investigation seems warranted.

A frequent argument in favor of infanticide is the almost prohibitively high cost of neonatal care and subsequent rehabilitation or maintenance of disabled children. A recent headline, reporting on the research of Dr. Mitzi L. Duxbury, put the question starkly: "Choice between baby, bankruptcy."[43]

Dr. Duxbury, assistant of graduate studies at the University of Minnesota School of Nursing, is one of many who have called attention to the high cost of care for disabled newborns. Duxbury noted, for example, that to save a baby born weighing less than 2.2 pounds, the average cost is now $40,000, with problem cases breaking the $100,000 barrier. Only 30 percent of such children can be saved, she contends, and 15 to 25 percent of those have severe mental or physical disorders.[44]

Some persons have promoted infanticide in cases where costs of care are high, arguing that resources ought to be allocated elsewhere. Yet, as Princeton Professor Paul Ramsey argues, such decisions ought to be made when technologies are being developed (should technology X be developed or not?) rather than making a decision, in order to cut costs, to deny technology to a disabled child once it is generally available.[45] Once such technology is available, Ramsey contends, discrimination on expected quality-of-life considerations is illegitimate; disabled and "normal" infants needing similar care should be treated similarly whenever possible.[46]

The relevance of cost to the discussion of contemporary infanticide is that a "crisis" in resource availability seems to be upon us; that is, to many there is not sufficient health care to go around. In the face of such a crisis, those with the lowest quality-of-life expectations should be denied care when in competition (real or imagined) with "normal" children.

But does such a crisis in fact exist? Experts may not agree, but it seems clear that what is at issue is relative, not absolute, scarcity. American society is not, at this writing at least, faced with a life-or-death condition of radical overall scarcity. More accurately, the issue is how—and to whom— our finite health resources are to be distributed. This is not a new development; limits to care have always existed, determined, among other considerations, by society's ranking of health care in relation to competing claims on resources.

Even if such a desperate situation existed, however, selection on quality-of-life principles would not necessarily be the most equitable or the only option available. Ramsey suggests as alternatives:

> to assure equal opportunity to gain access to life-saving treatment when, tragically, not all can be saved. . . . a lottery system kidney dialysis [could be effected]; some such scheme would be better than resorting to the use of "social worthiness" criteria. . . . Shutting down the intensive care unit altogether—which I do not propose—would have at least this virtue: no preemie would have cause to complain that he or she was treated unfairly, unjustly, unequally. None would be let go because he or she was unwanted by parents or unneeded by society. No preemie would be compared with another at risk of flunking someone's expected-social-worthiness test.
>
> This extreme option illustrates the fact that under conditions that necessarily limit our capacity to save young lives, a policy of selectivity should be by broad categories if such a policy is going to acknowledge the equal and independent value of human lives.[47]

Perhaps a sense of perspective can be gained from an example one commentator uses regarding the costs of care for children with Down's syndrome, a frequent subject of infanticide discussions. Institutionalization, which is among the most expensive and least desirable means of caring for such children, in 1977 cost approximately $12,000 a year for each child. For the sake of discussion, assume that all of the approximately 5,000 children born that year with Down's syndrome were institutionalized (although most would not be). In that case, "we would be spending each year on their care about 1/10 of what we spend as a nation on dogfood."[48] The same author writes elsewhere that

> [o]ne is told that if we could only divert the money spent on the custodial care of retarded children into research and nutrition, that we would soon have both a cure for cancer and sirloin for every family in the inner city. Caring for retarded children and research and nu-

trition are not mutually exclusive. Who says, that in a trillion dollar economy, we can not do all three by shifting our priorities?[49]

Contemporary infanticide is unusual, at least in some aspects, because of its appeal to scarcity in a period of relative abundance. What may be to blame more than a scarcity of resources, it seems fair to suggest, is a scarcity of imagination regarding resource allocation and means of equitable distribution.

Although more historical research is needed before firm conclusions can be reached in this area, it seems plausible to suggest that the degree to which the professions have encouraged infanticide in recent years stands out in a culture still holding to a *pro forma* commitment to the integrity of human life. Professor Piers and others have commented on the tacit approval that elite groups have given to infanticide in the past,[50] but the actual degree of advocacy on behalf of infanticidal policies by professionals does not readily emerge from the relevant literature. And while in some cultures, principally those of a more primitive nature, societal leaders may engage in infanticide in some manner or another (infant sacrifice, for example), the current situation seems fundamentally different.

In medieval Europe the agents of infanticide were among the lowest and least reputable members of society—wet nurses, midwives, and others. In modern times, however, these agents are found among the most respected classes in society—physicians in particular. That the physician's role as an agent of infanticide is at odds with the traditional canons of medical ethics is apparent. Whether this new role will be seen as a historical abberation, or as part of a series of new functions that the medical profession will fulfill for society, can only be judged at a later date. Still, physicians do not act alone; their actions are tacitly acceded to by many members of the legal profession, who treat infanticide with "benign neglect," and by academicians from divergent backgrounds who provide justifications for the previously unjustifiable.

* * *

Infanticide is a practice with roots firmly planted in human experience. Discussions of its contemporary practice, or advocacy thereof, are hence incomplete without discussing it in historical and social context. We are aware, however, that by making reference to the antecedents of modern infanticide we may be inviting readers to conclude that past practices are justification for those of our age. Such a conclusion would, in our opinion, be wrong. Practices cannot be judged to be ethical or unethical solely by virtue of past experience. Were such the case, the atrocities of one age would live on as the justification of future crimes. Still, we feel that some knowledge of the antecedents of the practice of infanticide is helpful, if for no other reason than to indicate the enormity of the problem.

A more in-depth and complete evaluation of the social forces that have in the past encouraged, and continue to encourage, or condone, infanticide is a task that must fall to others. The authors do feel compelled to suggest, however, that caution be exercised lest the complexities of the justifications, motivations, and accommodations obscure the simplicity of the deed in question—the killing of a helpless child, no matter how impaired or imperfect.

And while further study remains to be done on many of the topics touched upon in this chapter, it seems safe to observe that, whatever else may differ over time, large-scale infanticide presents almost (but, alas, not quite) irreconcilable contradictions to Western societies based on principles of equal protection and justice. This is as true today as it has been in times past. Indeed, we would all be the worse should such contradictions disappear. For if a society accedes to infanticide without a struggle or protest, it has lost an ennobling sense of purpose, a loss as great as the loss of its children.

We would do well to remember that infirmity, in varying degrees and measures, is an irremovable piece of the human puzzle. To remove it by force, from the individual or from the larger society, is to do violence to the vulnerability we all share. The chains that bind us to one another—to those before us and to those who will follow—are weakest where our disadvantaged brothers and sisters confront us; ultimately, we cut such links at our own peril.

Notes

1. Langer, *Checks on Population Growth: 1750–1850,* 226 Scientific Am. 96 (1972).

2. M. Piers, Infanticide: Past and Present 63 (1978).

3. *Id.* at 75. *See also* O. Werner, The Unmarried Mother in German Literature 1 (1917).

4. O. Werner, *supra* note 3 at 25 *citing* Joseph Friesen, Geschichte des Canonischen Eherects bis zum Verfall der Glossenliteratur 687 (1888).

5. *Id.*

6. *Id.* at 28.

7. S. Smith, The Battered Child Syndrome 4 (1976).

8. O. Werner, *supra* note 3, at 19 *citing* W. Sumner, Folkways 317, 319 (1907).

9. Williamson, *Infanticide: An Anthropological Analysis,* in Infanticide and the Value of Life 64–65 (M. Kohl ed. 1978).

10. *See, e.g.,* L. Tiger, Men in Groups 213 (1969).

11. M. Piers, *supra* note 2, at 15.

12. *Id.* at 17.

13. Langer, *supra* note 1 at 98.

14. O. Werner, *supra* note 3, at 20.

15. M. PIERS, *supra* note 2, at 51.

16. Langer, *supra* note 1, at 97.

17. M. PIERS, *supra* note 2, at 45.

18. *Id.* at 122.

19. O. WERNER, *supra* note 3, at 9.

20. *Id.* at 6.

21. M. PIERS, *supra,* note 2, at 122.

22. Ryan, *Child-Murder in Its Sanitary and Social Bearings,* in SANITARY REVIEW AND JOURNAL OF PUBLIC HEALTH 15 (1868).

23. O. WERNER, *supra* note 3, at 107.

24. An Act for the Better Protection of Infant Life, 1872, 35 & 36 Vict. c. 38.

25. Current British regulations for infant care are governed by a statute passed in 1948. *See* Nurseries and Child-Minders Regulation Act, 1948, 11 & 12 Ges. 6 c. 53. 17 Halisbury's Stat. 583.

26. *See, e.g.,* Chapter 8. *See also* ETHICS OF NEWBORN INTENSIVE CARE (A. Jonsen & M. Garland eds. 1976); Duff & Campbell, *Moral and Ethical Dilemmas in the Special-Care Nursery,* 289 NEW ENGLAND J. MED. 890–94 (1973); Robertson, *Involuntary Euthanasia of Defective Newborns: A Legal Analysis,* 27 STAN. L. REV. 213–69 (1975).

27. English, *Correlates of Stigma Toward Physically Disabled Persons,* in REHABILITATION RESEARCH AND PRACTICE REVIEW (1971), *reprinted in* SOCIAL AND PSYCHOLOGICAL ASPECTS OF DISABILITY: A HANDBOOK FOR PRACTITIONERS 209 (J. Stubbins ed. 1977) [hereinafter cited as English, *Correlates of Stigma*].

28. *Id.* at 209–10.

29. Buscaglia, *Handicaps Are Made, Not Born,* in THE DISABLED AND THEIR PARENTS: A COUNSELING CHALLENGE II (L. Buscaglia ed. 1975).

30. English, *Correlates of Stigma, supra* note 27, at 220.

31. E. ROSKIES, ABNORMALITY AND NORMALITY: THE MOTHERING OF THALIDOMIDE CHILDREN 285 (1972).

32. *Id.* at 284.

33. ANGLICAN CHURCH OF CANADA, TASK FORCE ON HUMAN LIFE/INTERIM REPORT, *Dying: Considerations Concerning the Passage from Life to Death,* 14 (presented to General Synod Aug. 11–18, 1977). The Synod sent the report back to committee, amid widening controversy.

34. Diamond, *The Deformed Child's Right to Life,* in DEATH, DYING AND EUTHANASIA 130 (D. Horan & D. Mall eds. 1977) [hereinafter cited as Diamond, *The Deformed Child's Right to Life*].

35. Evans, *Our Attitudes Handicap the Disabled,* Detroit Free Press, Apr. 2, 1981, at 9A.

36. Diamond, *The Deformed Child's Right to Life, supra* note 34, at 130.

37. K. HULL, THE RIGHTS OF PHYSICALLY HANDICAPPED PEOPLE: AN AMERICAN CIVIL LIBERTIES UNION HANDBOOK 22 (1979).

38. TenBroek, *The Right to Live in the World: The Disabled in the Law of Torts*, 54 CAL. L. REV 841–842 (1966).

39. Burt, *Authorizing Death for Anomalous Newborns*, in GENETICS AND THE LAW 441–42 (Milunsky & Annas eds. 1976).

40. Marks, *The Defective Newborn: An Analytic Framework for a Policy Dialog*, in ETHICS OF NEWBORN INTENSIVE CARE 103 (A. Jonsen & M. Garland eds. 1976).

41. *See, e.g., Retarded: The Overriding Picture Is That They Are Human*, Detroit Free Press, Apr. 5, 1981, at 28.

42. Ney, *Relationship Between Abortion and Child Abuse*, 24 CANADIAN J. PSYCH. 610–18 (1979).

43. State Journal (Lansing, Mich.), Mar. 22, 1981, D at 4.

44. *Id.*

45. P. RAMSEY, ETHICS AT THE EDGES OF LIFE 254–67 (1978).

46. *Id.* at 264.

47. *Id.* at 261–62.

48. Diamond, *The Deformed Child's Right to Life, supra* note 34, at 129.

49. *Id.* at 133.

50. M. PIERS, *supra* note 2, at 122.

2
Legal Aspects of Withholding Medical Treatment from Handicapped Children

John A. Robertson

Withholding necessary medical care from defective newborns in order to cause their death is a common practice in many medical centers across the United States. Noted doctors have described their practices of withholding care in the *New England Journal of Medicine*[1] and before Congress.[2] Other physicians have reported that they would not do a routine surgical procedure to remove a life-threatening intestinal blockage in retarded children, though they would in normal children.[3] Indeed, Drs. Joseph Goldstein, Anna Freud, and Albert Solnit assert in their influential *Before the Best Interests of the Child* that parents should be able to refuse necessary medical care for a child who has no "opportunity for either a life worth living or a life of relatively normal healthy growth."[4]

An important feature of this practice is its haphazard and often arbitrary occurrence. The frequency of conditions that call forth nonconsensual passive euthanasia of defective newborns varies with the hospital and the parents and doctors involved. In most instances there are no written rules or guidelines. Either the parent or doctor will suggest nontreatment, depending on their view of the severity of the case. It is not unknown, however, to have children with relatively mild defects, such as Down's syndrome[5] or low-lesion meningomyelocele,[6] to be selected for nontreatment, as well as those who have very severe brain damage[7] or who will die in a few days, weeks, or months despite very aggressive medical care.

Doctors involved in care of such newborns have often recommended the widest possible discretion for parents and physicians facing these choices. For example, Drs. Raymond S. Duff and A. G. M. Campbell, who publicized this practice at the Yale-New Haven Hospital in a famous article in the *New England Journal of Medicine,* have recommended that

John A. Robertson received his B.A. from Dartmouth and his J.D. from Harvard. He is currently Professor, University of Wisconsin Law School, and Professor, Program in Medical Ethics, University of Wisconsin Medical School. He is the author of *The Rights of the Critically Ill.*

the burdens of decision making must be borne by families and their professional advisers because they are most familiar with the respective situations. Since families primarily must live with and are most affected by the decisions, it therefore appears that society and the health professions should provide only general guidelines for decision making. Moreover, since variations between situations are so great, and the situations themselves so complex, it follows that much latitude in decision making should be expected and tolerated.[8]

No doubt much of the leeway claimed for parents in these decisions comes from a firm tradition of giving parents freedom in raising their children. Sometimes spoken of as the "natural rights of parents," parental decisions concerning the child's education, life-style, medical care, and well-being is, in our system, one that depends in the first instance on the dictates of the parents' conscience, and not on state or public views of what is good for the child.

Although the commitment to parental authority is a strong one, it is also well settled that parental rights over their children are not absolute. The parental right to control a child's nurture is not an absolute property right that can be enforced to the detriment of the child, but rather "is akin to a trust subject to ... a correlative duty to care for and protect the child"[9] that is terminable by the parents' failure to discharge their obligations. Thus, when parental conduct threatens a child's well-being in a significant way, the interests of the state and of the individual child may mandate intervention, although the state has a heavy burden of justification before abridging parental autonomy.[10]

The grounds for state intervention in child rearing are well established. When the child is abused or neglected, is denied education, or is denied necessary medical care, there is little question that parental rights give way to the child's right to a healthy development and well-being, even when the parental wishes are grounded in deeply held religious views.[11] A classic statement of this position arose in a case in which parents who were Jehovah's Witnesses had refused permission for blood to be transfused to a seriously ill child.

> The right to practice religion freely does not include the liberty to expose ... a child ... to ill health or death. Parents may be free to become martyrs themselves. But it does not follow that they are free, in identical circumstances, to make martyrs of their children before they have reached the age of full and legal discretion when they can make that choice for themselves.[12]

A second factor in the practice is the great sympathy we can feel for parents of a seriously defective child. They were looking forward to a healthy baby and suddenly are told that the infant is not "normal," is seriously ill or deformed, may not live, or may not develop into a healthy child. We can empathize with the shock, grief, anger, guilt, and resentment that they feel at the birth of such a child, and understand their feeling that they would never be able to cope with the financial costs or physical and psychological stresses of caring for such a child at home.

Behind these sympathies, however, may lie a bias against or dislike of the physically and mentally handicapped. Care of the handicapped does present substantial burdens to parents, family, and even taxpayers. It draws upon depths of care and concern that many people lack or fear that they lack. The very existence of such children is a grim reminder of our own dependency, and the way in which our own lives may be twisted irreparably by fate.

The tradition of parental authority, sympathy for the parents, and dislike of the handicapped may explain the practice of passive euthanasia of defective newborns, but it hardly legitimizes it. Indeed, the legality of the practice deserves close attention, for it involves decisions by the caretakers of vulnerable infants intended to cause their death. In this chapter I will describe the possible legal consequences that could arise when parents decide against necessary medical treatment of a handicapped child, and doctors and nurses acquiesce, and then describe the circumstances in which withholding treatment of severely defective newborns should be legally recognized.

The legal question may be considered from the perspective of the physician and parents faced with the decision to provide or withhold an essential life-saving medical procedure to a child with Down's syndrome or meningomyelocele, such as repair of a duodenal atresia, or closing of the lesion on the child's spine. May the parents ever legally refuse necessary treatments for children in that situation? May the doctor legally decide not to treat when the parents request it? What if the doctor wants to treat and the parents say no? What if the parents want to treat and the doctor says no? To answer these questions let us consider two situations in which questions of legality could arise: criminal prosecution for nontreatment, and court authorization to treat when the parents refuse.

One way to understand the legality of the practice of passive euthanasia of defective newborns is to ask whether the law would allow criminal prosecution of the parents and doctor. Could a district attorney legally bring charges? Could a jury legally convict parents and doctors of a crime for failing to treat? Although the courts have not directly addressed these questions, a reasonably clear answer may be extrapolated from the general law of crimes.

Since the law takes a patient-centered approach to treatment decisions involving children, parents and doctors who withhold necessary medical care from a newborn in order to cause its death could be prosecuted for several crimes, ranging from homicide to child abuse and conspiracy.

Generally, homicide by omission occurs when a person's failure to discharge a legal duty to another person causes that person's death.[13] If the required action is intentionally withheld, the crime is either first- or second-degree murder, depending on the extent of premeditation and deliberation.[14] Omissions through gross carelessness or disregard of the consequences of failing to act, are charged with involuntary manslaughter.[15]

In the case of a defective infant the withholding of essential care would appear to present a possible case of homicide by omission on the part of parents, physicians, and nurses, with the degree of homicide depending on the intent and extent of premeditation. Following a live birth, the law presumes that personhood exists and that there is entitlement to the usual legal protections, whatever the specific physical and mental characteristics of the infant may be.[16] Every state imposes on parents a legal duty to provide necessary medical assistance to a helpless minor child.[17] If they withhold such care and the child dies, they may be prosecuted for manslaughter or murder, as has frequently occurred when parents have refused or neglected to obtain medical care for nondefective children.[18] There is no reason why this rule would not apply equally to many cases of nontreatment of defective infants. Defenses based on religious grounds, or even on poverty, if public assistance is available, have been specifically rejected, and other legal defenses, such as the defense of necessity, may not apply.[19] While care may be omitted as "extraordinary" if there is only a minimal chance of survival, when survival is likely, treatment cannot be withheld simply because of cost or the future social disutility of the infant.[20]

In addition to homicide, parents may also be liable under statutes that make it criminal for a parent to neglect to support or to provide necessities, to fail to furnish medical attention, to maltreat, to be cruel to, or to endanger the child's life or health.[21]

The attending physician who counsels the parents to withhold treatment, or who merely acquiesces in their decision and takes no steps to save the child's life, may also incur criminal liability. Since withholding needed medical care by the parents would in many states constitute child abuse or neglect, the physician who knows of the situation and fails to report the case to proper authorities would commit a crime in the twenty or so states where failure to report child abuse is a crime.[22] While failure to report is only a misdemeanor, under the common law "misdemeanor-manslaughter rule" a person whose misdemeanor causes the death of another is guilty of manslaughter.[23] Since reporting might have led to appointment of a guardian and thus saved the child's life, the physician who fails to report could be guilty of manslaughter.

The physician may also be guilty of homicide by omission because he has breached a legal duty to care for the child and thereby caused the child's death. The legal duty of the physician is to intervene directly in an emergency by carrying out the procedure, or in other cases to report the case to public or judicial authorities who may then intervene to save the child. The sources of this duty are several. One is the child abuse reporting statutes, which impose a legal duty to report instances of parental neglect even in those states where failure to report is not criminal.

The duty may also derive from the physician's initial undertaking of care of the child. Although it may appear that by refusing consent the parents have terminated the physician's legal duty to care for the child, there are at least three possible grounds for arguing that the parents are not able to terminate the physician's obligations to the infant-patient—once the doctor-patient relationship has begun—if the patient will be substantially harmed by his withdrawal.

The first argument is based on the law of contract. The attending physician has contracted with the parents to provide care for a third party, the infant. Ordinarily the contract for services will be made with an obstetrician, a general practitioner, and/or a pediatrician before or at birth to provide all necessary medical care. When the child is born, this contractual obligation to provide services begins. Under the law of third party beneficiary contracts, the parties contracting for services to another cannot terminate the obligation to a minor if the minor would be thereby substantially harmed.[24] Since the parents are powerless to terminate the physician's obligation to care for the child, the physician would have a legal duty to take such steps as are necessary to protect the interests of the child. If emergency treatment were required, the physician would be privileged to proceed without parental consent.[25] In most cases (where feasible) the physician's duty would be better fulfilled by seeking the appointment of a guardian who could then consent to treatment.

The attending physician's contractual duty to care for the child despite parental denial of consent would not exist if the physician clearly agreed to treat the child only if normal, or, if the parents in engaging the physician made their agreement subject to modification in case of a defective birth.[26] However, neither parents nor physicians are likely in prenatal consultations to be so specific. Prosecution could, of course, change prevailing practices.

Second, even if the contract theory were rejected, physicians would still have a legal duty to care for the child on the traditional tort doctrine that one who assumes the care of another, whether gratuitously or not, cannot terminate such care if the third person would be hurt thereby.[27] This rule is based on the idea that one who undertakes care prevents others who might have come to the infant's aid from doing so.[28] Again, the physician could withdraw or not treat only if he has taken steps to notify public or hospital authorities, who would protect the child by pursuing the appointment of a guardian.

Third, it could also be argued that the physician would have a legal duty to protect the child on the ground that he has placed the child in peril through his role as a source of information for the parents. A person who puts another in peril, even innocently and without malice, incurs a legal duty to act to protect the imperiled person.[29] By giving the parents adverse prognostic information regarding the infant's handicaps, the economic and psychological burdens to be faced by the parents, and so on, he may be the immediate cause of nontreatment of the infant by leading the parents to a decision they would not otherwise have made or perhaps even considered. Under this theory even a consultant might be liable if he communicated information that led to a nontreatment decision and death, particularly if the information was incorrect or unfairly presented and then he took no action to save the child.[30]

In addition to liability for homicide by omission or under the misdemeanor-manslaughter rule, the physician may also be subject to homicide liability as an accessory—an accessory being a person who "counsels, encourages or aids or abets another to commit a felony."[31] This would be clearest in a case in which the physician counseled or encouraged the parents to withhold treatment. If omission of care by the parent is criminal, then the physician's liability as an accessory follows. If the physician were indifferent to the child's fate, or preferred that it would live but felt obligated to provide the parents with all the facts, it is less likely he would be culpable, since the requisite intent would be lacking.[32]

The attending physician may be guilty of conspiracy to commit homicide or violate the child abuse or neglect laws. Conspiracy is an agreement between two or more parties to achieve an unlawful objective, with (in most jurisdictions) an overt action toward that end.[33] If parents and physician agree that a defective newborn infant should die, and take any action toward that end, conspiracy could exist. Similarly, a staff conference on a particular case could amount to conspiracy, if the attending physician and others agreed that medical or surgical procedures should be withheld from the child.[34]

Physicians other than the attending physician, such as consultants, house officers, and administrative personnel, might also incur criminal liability under the statutes and common law principles reviewed above.

Nurses who participate or acquiesce in parental decisions to withhold treatment may also be at risk. While a nurse's care is subordinate to the orders of a physician, her legal duty is not fulfilled simply by carrying out physician orders with requisite skill and judgment. In some cases she is required to act independently or directly counter to the physician, if protection of the patient requires it.[35] At the very least, she might be obligated to inform her supervisor. A finding consistent with this view was reached in *Goff v. Doctors Gen. Hosp.*[36] where two nurses, the attending physician, and the hospital were held civilly liable when a patient died from postpartum cervical hemorrhage. The nurses were aware the mother was in peril but did not contact the attending physician because they thought he would not come. The court found that they had a duty to report the situation to a superior.

The existence of potential criminal liability is no guarantee that parents, physicians, nurses, and hospitals will in fact be prosecuted, nor that any prosecution will succeed. While parents and doctors who have actively killed patients have been prosecuted (though sometimes acquitted),[37] until recently no parent or physician has been prosecuted for withholding care from a defective newborn infant.[38] The dearth of prosecutions may be explained by lack of publicity about the practice, by limited prosecutorial resources, by a perception that the community tolerates the practice, or by a feeling that the situation is a tragic one that prosecution will not aid.

The infrequency of past criminal prosecutions, however, may not be a reliable guide to the future. As nontreatment practices become more visible, community pressure to prosecute, at least in egregious cases, may develop. Groups concerned about the sanctity of life and the interests of handicapped persons have begun to take an interest in the issue and may support or demand enforcement of the law by prosecutors.

That the threat of prosecution is no longer hypothetical was made clear in Danville, Illinois, in 1981, where a district attorney for the first time filed charges against parents and three attending physicians for nontreatment of a defective newborn.[39] The case arose when Siamese twins jointed at the waist were born on May 6, 1981 to a nurse and doctor who, allegedly with the anesthesiologist, obstetrician, and family doctor present at the birth, agreed not to treat or feed the babies. The twins were taken to the newborn nursery and left to die. The nurses on the ward became uncomfortable; at least one fed the babies several times. Complaints were made to the attending physician. On May 13 an anonymous telephone caller told the Illinois Department of Children and Family Services that Siamese twins at Lakeview Medical Center in Danville were being neglected. A social worker investigated. On May 15 Family Services filed a petition of neglect against the parents, asking that the department be given custody of the children. After a hearing at which several nurses testified, the judge found that the infants had been neglected during the eight-day stay, and ordered that temporary custody be given to Family Services. The twins were moved to Children's Memorial Hospital in Chicago for evaluation and treatment.

On June 11 the district attorney of Vermilion County, Illinois, filed criminal charges against the parents and the attending physician for conspiracy to commit murder and endangering the life and health of children. This was the first time that criminal charges had ever been filed against parents and doctors for withholding food or medical treatment from a newborn with major birth defects. On July 17 a preliminary hearing was held to ascertain whether there was probable cause that the defendants had committed the crime. At the hearing none of the nurses was willing or able to link the parents and physician directly with orders to withhold food from the twins. Based on the lack of evidence, the judge found no probable cause and dismissed the charges.

Because there is moral conflict and controversy over nontreatment decisions, criminal prosecution of parents and physicians for nontreatment of handicapped newborns will be viewed by many as a drastic remedy that should be used carefully and sparingly. In retrospect, the Danville case may have been too hastily brought. The criminal charges were filed before it was determined that surgical separation of the twins was not medically feasible and that their chances of survival were not good. Moreover, prosecution was not necessary to secure treatment since a custody order requiring treatment had already been made.[40]

Although criminal prosecution could deter nontreatment decisions, many people would agree that the interests of handicapped newborns would be better protected by physicians becoming more sensitive to the child's interest and by custody and neglect proceedings rather than by the heavy hand of criminal law. Prosecution, if it occurs at all, should be a last resort, reserved for the most flagrant cases where the violation of rights is clearest. Ill-considered prosecutions will only lead to acquittals, and a community backlash that could lead ultimately to even less respect for the rights of the handicapped.

The legality of withholding treatment from defective newborns may also be raised in a petition to a court to treat the child over the parents' objections. Doctors (or the hospital) may seek authority to treat for two reasons. The doctors might disagree with the parents' decision and think that the child should be treated. Or they might be fearful of legal liability and want to be sure that withholding treatment is legally justified.

In such a proceeding a court is likely to authorize treatment, for the law generally protects all persons equally, regardless of their physical and mental handicaps. Thus, in the 1974 Houle case in Maine,[41] when parents refused consent to a repair of a tracheal esophageal fistula on a convulsive newborn child who had some unknown measure of brain damage, no left eye or ear, and a malformed left thumb, the court had no hesitancy in issuing an order for treatment.

[A]t the moment of live birth there does exist a human being entitled to the fullest protection of the law. The most basic right enjoyed by every human being is the right to life itself. . . . The issue before the court is not the prospective quality of the life to be preserved, but the medical feasibility of the proposed treatment compared with the almost certain risk of death should treatment be withheld. Being satisfied that corrective surgery is medically necessary and medically feasible, the court finds that the defendants herein have no right to withhold such treatment and that to do so constitutes neglect in the legal sense.[42]

Similarly, in a recent New York case involving a newborn girl with meningomyelocele, the court granted the hospital's petition to be appointed guardian for the purpose of consenting to repair of the meningomyelocele.[43] The parents had refused consent for surgery to close the lesion on the back, and insisted on taking the child home to "let God decide" if the child is to live or die.[44] At the time the extent of the child's handicaps from the meningomyelocele were not known. However, since the lesion was very low on the spinal column, it appeared likely that she could be ambulatory with braces and would have normal intellectual development, though she would have no bowel or bladder control and might need a cranial shunt in case of hydrocephalus. The court had no difficulty in ordering treatment, for the child "has a reasonable chance to live a useful, fulfilled life,"[45] and the petition asked "that a child born with handicaps be given a reasonable opportunity to live, to grow and hopefully to surmount those handicaps."[46] The court emphasized that it was not confronting a "hopeless life,"[47] and did not indicate how it would rule in such a case.

Courts have occasionally deviated from the long tradition of protecting the life of a handicapped child who would clearly benefit from treatment.[48] (There is a class of treatment decisions, discussed below, in which refusal of the petition is justified in terms of the child's own interests.) Two such cases arose recently which have gained wide publicity. Both cases involved refusing surgical procedures on children with Down's syndrome. Since persons with Down's syndrome may be only mildly or moderately retarded, are educable, and may be able to do sheltered work and live happy lives, it is very difficult to justify nontreatment as serving their interest.

The "Infant Doe" case arose in April 1982 when a baby boy was born with Down's syndrome and a tracheal esophagal fistula (an opening between the windpipe and esophagus that prevents food from getting to the stomach) in Bloomington, Indiana.[49] The parents refused to allow intravenous feeding and surgery to repair the esophagus. The hopsital sought a court hearing to determine the legality of the parents' action. A juvenile court judge ruled that the parents could refuse the surgery and thus cause the child's death. The Indiana Supreme Court refused to hear the matter on appeal. The baby died before an appeal could be taken to the U.S. Supreme Court. From the facts that are known (the hearing was closed and the judge issued no opinion), the case appears to elevate inappropriately the parents' interest in having the child die immediately (rather than be adopted or raised in an institution) over the child's interest in life. It deviates from the strong current of precedent in this area, and because it is a trial judge's decision without opinion, it will have little precedential value.

The Becker case,[50] a decision by an intermediate appellate court in California also is difficult to justify in terms of the child's interest.

Phillip Becker is a twelve-year-old boy who is mildly retarded as a result of Down's syndrome. His IQ is about 60; he is educable, can communicate verbally, can tend to many of his needs, and can work in a sheltered workshop setting. His parents never took him home after his birth, though they visit him occasionally in the private group residence in which he lives. His living expenses are paid for by the state of California.

A routine medical examination revealed that Phillip was suffering from a ventricular septal defect—a not uncommon cardiac defect that involves a hole between two chambers of the heart. If the defect is repaired, which usually occurs early in a child's life when it is first noticed, he will have normal longevity. If it is not repaired, he will slowly deteriorate with the heart forced to work harder, eventually pumping unoxygenated blood through the body. During the later course of illness he will be unable to engage in minimal exertions such as walking, will be gasping for breath, and will eventually die from lack of oxygen to his body.

Although advised of this possibility, the parents refused consent to the operation needed to repair the defect. The persons caring for him informed the state child welfare authorities, who brought a petition asking that he be found neglected and that a guardian be appointed to consent to the surgery. After a hearing before a trial judge, the judge rejected the petition. On appeal to the California intermediate appellate court, the Court of Appeals, this decision was affirmed.[51] Petitions for discretionary further review to the California and United States Supreme Courts were rejected.[52]

The Becker decision does not withstand critical scrutiny, and for that reason is unlikely to be a precedent followed by other courts that carefully consider the issue. (Indeed, it has binding effect only within the fourth appellate district of California—the San Francisco Bay area). The decision cannot be cogently rationalized as serving the child's interest. Although there is a 5 percent risk of mortality from the surgery, and postoperative complications are more likely than in the case of a normal child,[53] it is very difficult to argue that the operation is not in Phillip's interest. Without it he is certain to die a slow, painful death in the next five to ten years, with the last years full of agony and suffering. With it he is assured a long life of ordinary health. Although the surgical risk is significant, it is not so high that reasonable people would reject the operation. Indeed it is widely recognized that if Phillip were normal, the operation would clearly be seen to be in his interests.

The parents stated that they opposed the operation because they were concerned that he might be institutionalized after their death. But this concern hardly seems to justify denying him a procedure without which he is sure to die in the next several years. Unless life in an institution was so horrible that death was preferable, the parents' concern would not justify denying him such a necessary medical procedure. Nor is the risk of the surgery so great relative to the benefits that the decision should be left to parental discretion.

One surmises that neither the parents nor the court gave due regard to the interests of the child, and instead were swayed by uncritical scrutiny of claims of parental autonomy, and perhaps a bias or prejudice against the retarded. Given the factual record developed in the trial court, it is especially disturbing that the decision was affirmed by the only appellate court to review the case. The California Court of Appeals upheld the decision on the narrow ground that there was not clear and convincing evidence that refusing the surgery amounted to neglect. The court seemed to have viewed the operation as more risky and less clearly beneficial than the trial court testimony indicated, and thus within the range of parental discretion. But the decision is difficult to justify on precisely those grounds, since the alternative to the not insubstantial risks of the operation is a sure and agonizing death in a much shorter time than the most optimistic figure (20 years) cited by the court.

Although it is likely that the courts would find a legal duty to treat most children with Down's syndrome and meningomyelocele, it would be a mistake to think that treatment would be legally required for all defective children, regardless of the severity of their defects. Although life is ordinarily a good for the person, even if the person is severely handicapped and might spend his life in an institution, it is not always nor necessarily a good. The situation may be such that, viewed solely from the perspective of the patient, further life is not in a patient's interests; his life is so full of pain and suffering that the burdens to him of the medical care necessary to keep him alive do not seem worth it. When adults find themselves in this situation and decline further care, we respect their choices. When they are incompetent and cannot speak for themselves, we make such choices for them. There is no reason why the same decision cannot be made with severely deformed newborns, as long as it proceeds truly and authentically from concern for them and not concern for others. Respect for life means that we show equal respect for the lives of the mentally and physically handicapped. It does not mean that all human life must be preserved whatever the cost, circumstances, or condition of the patient.

To understand how these principles apply to the situation of withholding treatment of defective newborns, consider the following situation that confronted pediatricians and neonatalogists recently at a major academic medical center. A baby boy born seven weeks premature, with a weight of 900 grams, had severe respiratory problems that led to bronchopulmonary dysplasia. Intracranial bleeding during this period caused irreversible brain damage that made development beyond the most minimal level highly unlikely. He was still respirator dependent at five months after birth, and his prognosis at that point, even with the most aggressive medical care, was very poor. The parents insisted that further care be stopped, and eventually the doctors acquiesced. The respirator was removed and he died.[54]

It seems to me that the legality of this action is very different from our analysis of the law involving nontreatment of children with Down's syndrome or meningomyelocele. Not only is prosecution more unlikely here than in those cases, if it were brought to trial the chances are very great

that a jury/court would find that the child's rights had not been violated—
that there was no duty to treat—on the basis of the principles discussed
above. This is because in this case it is very difficult to argue that further
living, from the child's perspective, serves his interest. First, the brain damage may be so severe that it may not be meaningful to speak of the child as
having interests. We do not, for example, find it easily comprehensible to
talk about people in chronic vegetative states as having interests. At the
bottom end of the IQ scale, as with encephalic or severely brain damaged
children, the same may be true.

But if this infant has interests, it has an interest in life only if that life
holds some good for it. If his life will be one of irremediable pain and suffering, then he may have no interest in staying alive. This is particularly
true if the infant's life expectancy is very short, as if he would survive only
a few weeks or months even with the most aggressive treatment.

It is important to recognize the source of the judgment being made
here. It does not arise out of concern for the interest of others, nor is it
based on the judgment that severe handicaps alone deprive a child of an interest in living. Instead, it is a patient-centered approach that focuses solely
on the needs and interests of the child, from the child's perspective as best
we can understand or infer it. Indeed, its scrupulous concern with the interests of the child means that very few cases meeting this criteria will be
found. There are few conditions so disabling that we can say with reasonable certainty that from the infant's perspective continued living is a fate
worse than death.

For example, most cases of Down's syndrome and meningomyelocele,
though they involve hydrocephalus, kyphoscoliosis, incontinence, non-
ambulation, and mental retardation, do not fit this category.[55] These infants may suffer from repeated medical interventions, and may not have access to the full range of opportunities of ordinary people. But the
perspective of the healthy, normal individual is the wrong perspective to
take. The view of ordinary people who know ordinary capacities for experience and interaction, and who may view the infant's existence as a fate
worse than death, does not tell us how the infant who has no other life experience would view it. For him life in a severely disabled form would
seem better than no life at all, even if his life is lived in the custodial wards
of a state institution.

However, where the child's existence would involve incessant, unreliev-
able pain; or is devoid of any possibility of realizing even the most minimal experience or states of being that make life for even the most disabled
person good; or, with lesser degrees of pain, where death is imminent and
unavoidable; a judgment that treatment is not, from the child's perspective, in his interests seems justified. Such judgments can be limited to
these extreme cases without spillover into situations where treatment is
warranted. Even physicians who are the most maximally committed to
preservation of life recognize that at some point further treatment hurts,

rather than advances, the interest of the patient.[56] Zealous concern for the rights of handicapped children should not blind one to the fact that there are cases where further medical procedures which could prolong a child's life may be omitted.

In such cases it is very unlikely that prosecution of the parents and doctors would be successful, or that a petition to authorize treatment would be granted. There is growing legal precedent for withholding care from adult patients in such circumstances. State supreme courts in New Jersey,[57] Massachusetts,[58] and New York[59] have recently faced this question in situations involving adult patients who were chronically vegetative, chronically senile, or profoundly retarded. The courts granted petitions for authorization to withhold medical procedures that could prolong their lives based on a patient-centered approach that gave priority to the interests and needs of the patient. Although the courts' reasoning in these cases has not always been consistent or cogent, it is clear that a legal consensus is developing that would authorize withholding medical procedures from incompetent adult patients when it reasonably appears that it is no longer in their interest to be treated. There is no reason why the principles underlying these precedents should not also apply to treatment decisions involving children who are in equally dire circumstances.

The law's emphasis on a patient-centered approach to withholding treatment from patients incapable of deciding for themselves protects the interest of most handicapped newborns in receiving medical treatment essential to their survival and the realization of whatever potential they have. Thus, legal analysis of the nontreatment decision shows that many, perhaps most, instances of nontreatment of handicapped newborns are illegal. The wishes of parents to allow such children to die can be overridden by judicial authorization of treatment. In egregious cases, parents, and the doctors and nurses who acquiesce in their decision, could be prosecuted for a variety of crimes connected with the nontreatment decision, though in the current climate prosecutions are unlikely, and in most instances may not be the best way to deal with this difficult situation.

The illegality and immorality of many nontreatment decisions should not, however, be interpreted to mean that all such decisions are necessarily illegitimate. In some extreme cases omission of further medical treatment may be the best alternative for the child, from the child's own perspective. Although the courts have not yet drawn clear lines defining those situations, the principles now evolving for withholding treatment from incompetent adults should apply to infants as well. Our concern for the wellbeing of handicapped newborns need not blind us to the situations in which respect for them requires that further medical procedures be stopped. While the consequences of error in either direction are great, there is no escape from the moral and legal duty of respecting the wellbeing and rights of the handicapped child.

Notes

1. Duff & Campbell, *Moral and Ethical Dilemmas in the Special-Care Nursery,* 289 NEW ENGLAND J. MED. 890 (1973).

2. *See, e.g.,* Robertson, *Involuntary Euthanasia of Defective Newborns: A Legal Analysis,* 27 STAN. L. REV. 213 (1975) [hereinafter cited as Robertson, *Involuntary Euthanasia*].

3. Todres, Krane, Howell, & Shannon, *Pediatricians' Attitudes Affecting Decision-Making in Defective Newborns,* 60 PEDIATRICS 197–201 (1977).

4. J. GOLDSTEIN, A. FREUD, & A. SOLNIT, BEFORE THE BEST INTERESTS OF THE CHILD 91–92 (1979).

5. Duff & Campbell, *supra* note 1, at 891.

6. *Id.* at 892.

7. *In re* Quinlan, 70 N.J. 10, 355 A.2d 647 (1976).

8. Duff & Campbell, *supra* note 1, at 894.

9. Custody of a Minor, 375 Mass. 733, 748, 379 N.E.2d 1053, 1063 (1978).

10. *Id.* at 749, 379 N.E.2d at 1063.

11. Wald, *State Intervention on Behalf of 'Neglected' Children: A Search for Realistic Standards,* 27 STAN. L. REV. 985 (1975).

12. People *ex rel.* Wallace v. Labrenz, 411 Ill. 618, 626, 104 N.E.2d 769, 774 (1952) (*citing* Prince v. Massachusetts, 321 U.S. 158, 166, 170 [1944]).

13. Robertson, *Medical Ethics in the Courtroom,* 4 HASTINGS CENTER REP. 1 (1974) [hereinafter cited as Robertson, *Medical Ethics*].

14. *Id.*; W. LAFAVE & A. SCOTT, HANDBOOK ON CRIMINAL LAW 190 (1972).

15. Robertson, *Medical Ethics, supra* note 13; W. LAFAVE & A. SCOTT, *supra* note 14, at 190.

16. People v. Chavez, 77 Cal. App. 2d 621, 176 P.2d 92 (1947); Robertson, *Medical Ethics, supra* note 13, at 1.

17. W. LAFAVE & A. SCOTT, *supra* note 14, at 182–91 (1972).

18. State v. Stehr, 92 Neb. 755, 139 N.W. 676 (1913); People v. Pierson, 176 N.Y. 201, 68 N.E. 243 (1903) (misdemeanor).

19. Stehr v. State, 92 Neb. 755, 760; 139 N.W. 676, 678 (1913) (poverty); People v. Pierson, 176 N.Y. 201, 210–12, 68 N.E. 243, 246–47 (1903) (religious grounds); Robertson, *Involuntary Euthanasia, supra* note 2, at 239.

20. Robertson, *Involuntary Euthanasia, supra* note 2, at 235.

21. *Id.* at 217–24.

22. *See, e.g.,* CAL. PENAL CODE 273a(1) (West 1970); VT. STAT. ANN. tit. 13, 1304 (1974).

23. W. LAFAVE & A. SCOTT, *supra* note 14, at 594–602.

24. *See, e.g.,* Rhodes v. Rhodes, 266 S.E.2d 790 (Ky. 1954); Plunkett v. Atkins, 371 P.2d 727 (Okla. 1962); Robertson, *Involuntary Euthanasia,* supra note 2, at 225.

25. Jackovach v. Yocom, 212 Iowa 914, 237 N.W. 444 (1931).

26. Rhodes v. Rhodes, 266 S.E.2d 790 (1954).

27. W. LaFave & A. Scott, *supra* note 14, at 185; W. Prosser, Law of Torts 343-48 (4th ed. 1971).

28. W. LaFave & A. Scott, *supra* note 14, at 185.

29. *Id.* at 186. *See also* Cal. Penal Code 273a(1) (West 1970); Vt. Stat. Ann. tit. 13, 1304 (1974).

30. Robertson, *Involuntary Euthanasia, supra* note 2, at 229-30.

31. W. LaFave & A. Scott, *supra* note 14, at 498.

32. Nye v. United States, 336 U.S. 613 (1949); Hicks v. United States, 395 F.2d 468 (8th Cir. 1968); Robertson, *Involuntary Euthanasia, supra* note 2, at 231-32.

33. Robertson, *Involuntary Euthanasia, supra* note 2, at 234.

34. *Id.*

35. *Id.* at 228 n.98.

36. 166 Cal. App. 2d 314, 333 P.2d 29 (1958).

37. Robertson, *Involuntary Euthanasia, supra* note 2, at 217 n.27.

38. *Id.* at 219.

39. *Id.* at 243-44.

40. *Id.* at 219 n.35, 243.

41. Maine Med. Center v. Houle, No. 74-145 Superior Court, Cumberland, Maine, dec. Feb. 14, 1974.

42. *Id.*

43. Application of Cicero, 101 Misc.2d 699, 421 N.Y.S.2d 965 (1979).

44. *Id.* at 700, 421 N.Y.S.2d at 966.

45. *Id.* at 702, 421 N.Y.S.2d at 968.

46. *Id.* at 701, 421 N.Y.S.2d at 967.

47. *Id.* at 702, 421 N.Y.S.2d at 968.

48. Robertson, *Involuntary Euthanasia, supra* note 2, at 268-69.

49. Boston Sunday Globe, Apr. 18, 1982.

50. *In re* Phillip B., 92 Cal. App. 3d 796, 156 Cal. Rptr. 48 (1979), *cert. denied sub nom.* Bothman v. Warren B., 445 U.S. 949 (1980).

51. 92 Cal. App. 3d 796, 156 Cal. Rptr. 48 (1979).

52. *See* Bothman v. Warren B., 445 U.S. 949 (1979). The Superior Court of Santa Clara County, California has given guardianship of the person of Phillip Becker to the couple, the Heaths, who sought to have the lifesaving surgery performed over the objections of Phillip's parents. Guardianship of Phillip Becker, No. 101981 (Aug. 7, 1981).

53. 92 Cal. App. 3d at 802, 256 Cal. Rptr. at 51.

54. [Report of case on file with author.]

55. J. Warkany, CONGENITAL MALFORMATIONS 272 (1971); Lorber, *Results of Treatment of Myelomeningocele,* 13 DEVELOPMENTAL MED. CHILD NEUROLOGY SUPPLEMENT 279-303 (1971).

56. For example, Dr. C. Everett Koop, a committed and compassionate defender of the rights of handicapped newborns, describes circumstances under which he will cease treatment on certain newborns. Koop, *Ethical and Surgical Considerations on the Care of the Newborn with Congenital Anomalies,* in chapter 8 of this volume.

57. *In re* Quinlan, 70 N.J. 10, 355 A.2d 647 (1976).

58. *In re* Spring, Mass., 405 N.E.2d 115 (1980); Superintendent of Belchertown v. Saikewicz, 3373 Mass. 728, 370 N.E.2d 417 (1977).

59. *In re* Storar, 52 N.Y.2d 363, 438 N.Y.S.2d 266, 420 N.E.2d 64 (1981). In this decision, the New York Court of Appeals decided the cases of John Storar, a 53 year old lifetime resident of state hospitals, and Brother Joseph Carles Fox, an 83 year old teacher who lapsed into a chronic vegetative coma following surgery. In the case of Brother Fox, the court affirmed the order to discontinue the use of the respirator, but substantially modified the opinion of the lower appellate court, which had formulated a constitutional "right to die" for terminally ill patients. Eichner v. Dillon, 73 A.D.2d 431, 458, 426 N.Y.S.2d 517, 539 (App. Div. 1980). In the case of John Storar, who was suffering from terminal cancer, the Court of Appeals reversed the lower court order which had authorized the discontinuance of blood transfusions. *In re* Storar, 78 A.D.2d 1013, 434 N.Y.S.2d 46 (1981).

3

The Doctor's Dilemma: Euthanasia, Wrongful Life, and the Handicapped Newborn

Dennis J. Horan and Steven R. Valentine

Infanticide of handicapped newborn infants through neglect or even by direct means has become a growing practice in hospitals across the United States.

At the same time that we contemplate the killing of handicapped children after birth we find that recent advances in prenatal diagnosis, which enable physicians to detect the presence of many genetic defects during pregnancy, make it possible to eliminate the handicapped child before birth through abortion. There is no doubt that the practice of destroying unborn handicapped infants, often referred to as "eugenic abortion," will increase with the institution of mass genetic screening programs of pregnant women.

At this time, however, American law is quite contradictory in its treatment of infanticide and eugenic abortion. Infanticide, whether through neglect, omission, or direct killing, is not legal and is subject to severe penalties under both the criminal and civil law. Eugenic abortion, however, like all abortion, was made legal as a matter of constitutional law by the Supreme Court's decision in *Roe v. Wade.* Furthermore, actions for "wrongful birth" have proliferated in American courts, wherein parents claim that, but for the failure of a physician to detect handicaps in prenatal diagnosis, the child born with defects would have been aborted. Such lawsuits may effectively require physicians to perform comprehensive prenatal screening for genetic defects and, if the mother desires, perform, or arrange for, a eugenic abortion. Physicians who fail to conduct tests to detect the presence

Dennis J. Horan received his B.S. and J.D. at Loyola University, Chicago. Currently he is a partner in the firm of Hinshaw, Culbertson, Moelman, Hoban, and Fuller, Chicago. He is also Lecturer in Medical Law at the University of Chicago. He is the former Chairman of the Medicine and Law Committee (TIPS Section) of the A.B.A.

Steven R. Valentine received his B.G.S. at Indiana University, where he is currently studying law. The author of *All Shall Live: Another Quaker Response to the Abortion Dilemma,* he is currently Executive Director, Americans United for Life, Chicago.

of a handicapped fetus are liable for massive damage awards to parents who claim that such a fetus would have been aborted had the doctor performed the relevant prenatal screening.

We are thus presented with a situation where the law (at least in form) offers severe punishment for the physician who abandons the handicapped born child to die while it virtually requires that the same physician conduct what some have labelled a "search and destroy mission" against the handicapped child in the womb.[1] This chapter first discusses the problem of the handicapped newborn and the legal remedies that are currently available to attack the practice of infanticide. We then turn to consideration of the actions for wrongful life and wrongful birth, and suggest a statutory remedy that will eliminate the present situation where physicians are severely sanctioned for not detecting and eliminating the handicapped before birth. Third, we examine the way in which current trends in American tort law may affect and encourage the practice of infanticide.

In an article in the *New England Journal of Medicine,* Medical Professors Raymond S. Duff and A. G. M. Campbell have raised for public discussion what they describe as moral and ethical dilemmas in the special care nursery.[2] Their article speaks of forty-three cases related to withholding treatment of defective newborns that resulted in their deaths. Those cases fall into the following categories: 15 multiple anomalies, 8 trisomy, 8 cardiopulmonary disease, 7 meningomyelocele, 3 central nervous system disorders, and 2 short bowel syndrome.

Drs. Duff and Campbell comment that: "After careful consideration of each of these 43 infants, parents and physicians in a group decision concluded that prognosis for meaningful life was extremely poor or hopeless and, therefore, rejected treatment."[3] Their paper was published in 1973, barely six months after the legalization of abortion by the United States Supreme Court. It is significant that Duff and Campbell use the same expression in their paper that the Court used in its abortion decision to demark the point of fetal viability: "meaningful life."[4] Duff and Campbell conclude their paper with the observation: "If working out these dilemmas in ways such as those we suggest is in violation of the law, we believe the law should be changed."[5]

At least one commentator has argued that the decision whether or not to treat the defective newborn should be made on the same basis as the abortion decision. His argument is that if the defective child, like the unborn child, is wanted by the parents, then treatment should be given. However, if the defective child is not wanted, then treatment should be withheld and the child allowed to die. The commentator who makes this argument finds his support, he contends, in *Roe v. Wade.*[6]

Roe v. Wade does not support the withholding of necessary medical care for the defective newborn. Reliance on that case to support such a proposition is misplaced and, indeed, contradictory since *Roe v. Wade* implies of necessity that at birth the constitutional right to life affixes and protects the born child. *Roe v. Wade* does not support death as a treatment of choice. That would be classified as euthanasia, which is a euphemism for homicide under American law and the laws of all nations.[7]

Professor John A. Robertson has done the most comprehensive legal analysis of withholding care from the defective newborn.[8] In his comments on the Duff and Campbell paper, Robertson points out how surprising it is that under these circumstances physicians, or anyone else, fail to inform the family of the legal rights and obligations involved in these problems and in the consideration of death as a possible solution. What those involved in the decision-making process should recall is that the born child is a person under the law, a constitutional person. Born children, no matter how defective, have the same rights under the criminal law and under the Constitution that you and I have. There seems to be a great deal of neglect in our society in transferring that information—those simple truths—to the parents involved in this decision. Indeed, in terms of the rights involved, one could consider that the defective child, under these circumstances, has more rights because he is dependent and possibly retarded, is immature, and consequently has a stronger moral claim on us for care than a healthy child.

The obligation to care for a child exists for the parents, the physician, and the hospital staff.[9] It may seem morally sensitive to declare that the decision of the family should be respected as final, but the fact of the matter is that the decision of the parent to withhold further treatment may not insulate or protect the physician and hospital or its personnel from potential liability, either civil or criminal.

In discussing these problems, we must first make the very necessary distinction of whether we are talking about a treatable or nontreatable case. Two of the children discussed in the Duff and Campbell paper died of short bowel syndrome where nontreatment was a matter of choice of both the physician and the parents. If there is no treatment for the condition, then our conscience, our moral feelings are not shocked or aroused by the fact that no treatment is given. Or, if in the medical judgment of the attending physician, the condition or conditions (for example, gross multiple anomalies) add up to a hopeless case, that is, the prognosis gives no prospect of recovery or relief from treatment, then withdrawal of the treatment, again, does not shock our conscience and does not bring into operation either the civil or criminal sanctions of the laws about which we speak.[10]

Withdrawal of treatment under those circumstances does not constitute abandonment of a patient, but the exercise of sound medical judgment based on only medical factors (not social), such as expected outcome and prognosis. The physician, under those circumstances, is not mandated to treat when treatment is useless. The standard of care requires of him only that he exercise the care and skill of ordinarily well-qualified physicians.

We are describing here the truly terminally defective infant in the new-born nursery who will die regardless of what ordinary or extraordinary means are used. It is not about these cases we are speaking when we discuss the potential criminal and civil liabilities surrounding the circumstances of withdrawal of treatment. We are talking about treatable cases where the prognosis is or may be guarded, but nonetheless an acceptable form of medical intervention exists that will correct the current condition of ill-being that otherwise would cause death.

In the Duff and Campbell paper we find one case that has been a "classic" in the literature, both legal and ethical, discussing the whole decision-making process that surrounds these very difficult cases. Duff and Campbell describe it thus:

> An infant with Down's Syndrome and intestinal atresia, like the much publicized one at Johns Hopkins Hospital, was not treated because his parents thought that surgery was wrong for their baby and themselves. He died several days after birth.[11]

In the Johns Hopkins case, which was reported in a film made years later by the Kennedy Foundation as a subject for these kinds of discussions, the child lived for fifteen days after the decision was made.[12] The decision to withhold treatment in that case has been universally criticized by ethical commentators in every field.

Professor Robertson has done a careful analysis of the legal liability surrounding that decision-making process.[13] He finds potential criminal liability for the parents as a result of such a decision and sees all the conditions being met for homicide by omission: first, the omission of a legal duty to protect another, which the parent has to the child; second, a willful or knowing failure to act, with knowledge of the probable result—withdrawal of treatment which will result in death; and third, the failure or omission is the probable cause of the child's death. If the omission is intentional, the result could be first- or second-degree murder; if the omission is careless or negligent (that is, if the state of mind of the people involved in the decision-making process is such that they are not capable of making a rational decision) it could be classified as gross negligence, the result being involuntary manslaughter.

In analyzing the problem it is probably better for our immediate purposes to set aside discussion of the parents and look at the potential liabilities from the point of view of the physicians, and hospital and support personnel, because their problem commences when the parents make a decision adverse to treatment.

One of the authors attended a seminar where neurosurgeons were involved, one of whom took a highly "technological" approach to the problem. His solution was: if the parents wanted the procedure done he would do it; if the parents did not want the procedure done he would not do it. Apparently, his own role as a moral person had little to do with his technological response to the problem.

The physician who withholds lifesaving treatment in the cases previously described (those cases where the prognosis is guarded, but the result can be good depending upon the outcome) may be found criminally culpable on two theories. First, if his withholding of care or his failure to report the case to appropriate authorities violates state neglect or child abuse reporting statutes, and the child dies, the physician may be guilty of involuntary manslaughter under the Misdemeanor-Manslaughter Rule. And second, the law imposes criminal liability for knowing or grossly negligent failure to provide care if that failure proximately caused the death of the person to whom the duty is owed.[14]

The physician and the hospital owe the duty because it arises out of the contractual relationship they have with the parents of the child. The physician and hospital agreed to render medical services and the parents agreed to pay for them. The services are for the benefit of the mother and the born child. When the parents withhold treatment, the issue as to consent for the treatment on behalf of the child arises. The important point is that the withholding of the consent to treatment by the parents under these circumstances does not extinguish the physician's or the hospital's obligation to continue to act on behalf of the child. What option is open to the physician and hospital when the parent refuses consent for treatment to the child? There is a practical option—it is to ask the parents to remove the child from the physician's care and the care of the institution. This is to say that the physician and the hospital resign from the case. Of course this does not solve the legal and ethical dilemma the physician has at that point because he has a duty imposed upon him by the child neglect and abuse laws to report such a case. He must struggle, then, with the problem of whether, even if the child is withdrawn from the hospital, he should inform the authorities that the child will not receive proper medical treatment. Another option in the face of the parents' refusal of consent is for the hospital to seek the courts' help in the appointment of a guardian who can then consent for the treatment on behalf of the child.

In addition to the criminal liability that may arise in these situations, tort law or personal injury law is applicable. In tort law the failure to treat can amount to the commission of a willful or intentional tort, or a negligent omission, or abandonment of the child.[15] The fact that the parents have consented to withdraw treatment does not protect the physician and the hospital. In other words, when sued by someone on the child's behalf for not having rendered treatment, which failure to treat resulted in the child's death, the hospital could not come into court and say "the parents wouldn't give us consent." As long as the child remains physically in the custody of the hospital—in one of its rooms, in one of its beds, under the care and treatment of one of its physicians—there is a responsibility that must be exercised. If the parents consented to withholding treatment, it would mean only that the parents would be barred from gaining from the action. If the child died, for example, there could be a cause of action known as wrongful death. The damages are measured by what we call loss of pecuniary support. What this means is that if there is any pecuniary loss involved (and when it is the death of a small child, the law often presumes pecuniary loss), that money, if any, would not go to parents who consented to withholding the treatment. They would be barred from recovery by their own act. That is not to say that some other member of the family who did not participate in withholding consent could not bring such an action. Indeed, if all family members were involved in withholding consent, then a public guardian could bring such an action.[16]

The potential criminal and personal injury or tort liability reinforce the conclusion that the legal and ethical dilemma for the physician and hospital really only begins when the parents make the judgment that they want to withhold treatment. How should the physician then conduct himself? His field is medicine. His expertise is in the exercise of medical judgment. When he stays in that field, when he exercises sound medical judgment based on a medical condition and then gives a judgment as to whether or not treatment should be withheld, he is acting in a safe, sound, and secure manner. When he makes that medical judgment based on a reasonable degree of medical and surgical certainty, concerned only with the prognosis of his patient—the child—he acts in the noblest manner as a professional. When he makes judgments that go beyond the use of his medical expertise, when he makes the kind of judgment that is made in the Duff and Campbell paper in those treatable cases, when he, in effect, determines that for social reasons some should live and some should die, he then is taking his medical boat out into the murky, troubling waters which have been described as the beginnings of the legalization of euthanasia.

In the case we have been discussing, ethical commentators such as James Gustafson[17] of the University of Chicago and Paul Ramsey of Princeton[18] conclude that the norm for treatment should be the same for the child with atresia and Down's syndrome as for the child with atresia who is otherwise normal and healthy. The same principle would be applicable to meningomyelocele: treatment should not be withheld for quality-of-life reasons. What is happening in these cases is that mental retardation is being looked upon by some people as a reason in and of itself for non-treatment at the option of the parents. That option creates another dilemma: the failure to feed. With the duodenal atresia or esophageal atresia, if you do not treat the condition how do you feed the child? Nothing can be taken by mouth, although intravenous feeding by gavage could maintain life optimally. Another option is not to feed, which option has universally been condemned by ethical commentators. The failure to treat the treatable cases leads to the dilemma of the failure to feed and the failure to feed leads to the dilemma of hastening death. Can the physician do that?

Hans Jonas puts the answer thus: "Now, as to outright hastening death by a lethal drug, the doctor cannot fairly be asked to make any of his ministrations for this purpose, nor the hospital staff to connive by looking the other way if someone else provides the patient the means. The law forbids it, but more so (the law being changeable) it is prohibited by the innermost meaning of the medical vocation, which should never cast the physician in the role of a dispenser of death, even at the subject's request."[19]

The legalization of abortion by the United States Supreme Court, however, has cast the physician in the role of the dispenser of death. When the court legalized abortion, in the minds of many judges, it made abortion legally normative just as is any other "medical procedure" required by the applicable standard of care.[20] Consequently, the failure of a physician to include abortion or abortion referral as a possible alternative to birth with handicaps may render him liable in tort to the defective child or its parents because of recent developments in American law.

The legalization of abortion and the newfound ability of the medical profession to diagnose most birth defects *in utero* have combined to produce the novel cause of action in tort law. "Wrongful life" has been coined by courts and commentators to describe distinct tort actions that seek the award of compensation for damages that arise from the birth of a handicapped child. When such a child sues on this ground, she does so on a claim of "wrongful life." When the parents[21] of a handicapped child bring suit on the same ground, their assertion is that of "wrongful birth."

The basic common element in these actions is the contention that the physician who is being sued has failed in his "duty" to conduct a pregnancy diagnostic test that would have led him to advise the parents involved of the significant possibility or likelihood of a serious birth defect. Both the wrongful life and wrongful birth lawsuits rest on the premise that had the parents known that their unborn child probably would be handicapped, the mother would have exercised the right to abort her. The very existence of the newborn defective child in such a case, then, is alleged to be the "fault" of the "negligent" medical practitioner.

The technological advances which make tenable this assignment of responsibility are of recent development. Until about a decade ago, the methods of detecting and predicting the most serious genetic birth defects were inexact and unreliable. Although not all such defects can be detected, many can be discovered in the fetus at the approximate gestational age of 15 weeks. More than sixty metabolic disorders,[22] as well as Down's syndrome, can be detected by amniocentesis[23] and/or ultrasonography.[24] Alpha-fetoprotein (AFP) analysis can be used to detect the presence of neural tube defects such as meningomyelocele (spina bifida) and anencephaly.[25] At present, there is no intrauterine treatment for neural tube disorders, or for Down's syndrome, two of the most common genetic defects.[26] Thus, if the goal of reduced incidence of birth defects is to be met, the consequence of prenatal screening will be the abortion of those fetuses that are found to be defective.

The mere availability of a medical procedure such as prenatal screening does not impose a legal duty upon physicians to perform that procedure in any given case. The omission of a procedure will only be found negligent if the court holds that the performance of that procedure was within the duty owed to the patient by the physician. The courts which have awarded damages for wrongful birth claims,[27] and the one court that has recognized an action for wrongful life,[28] have found that a physician who undertakes pregnancy care has a duty to assess genetic risk, to test and to test correctly, for fetal defects. These cases also hold that the physician has a concomitant duty to share the results of his diagnosis with the parents in genetic counseling. Two principal reasons are given for imposing these duties upon obstetricians. First, the performance of prenatal screening is necessary if a physician is to conform with the general level of practice within the obstetrics specialty, a standard which is set by physicians themselves.[29] Second, the provision of genetic counseling is necessary for a patient to make a truly informed consent to the decision whether to carry the pregnancy to term or obtain an abortion.[30] Thus, if a physician knew or should have known of facts that indicate a risk of a birth defect, he must disclose that knowledge so that parents may take it into account when considering whether to terminate the pregnancy.

Once such a duty has been established in the law of medical malpractice, the plaintiff must show that the physician's breach of that duty was a cause of the alleged injury or damage. In the wrongful life and wrongful birth causes of action, it is not contended that the physician's negligence in failing to fulfill his duty to disclose the genetic risk factor to the parents caused the child's handicap. Rather, it is asserted that his failure to so inform them was a proximate cause of the defective child's birth. In order to complete the chain of causation, then, it must be shown that, but for the physician's failure to inform, the mother would have exercised her right to end the pregnancy.

In seeking to establish the requisite proximate cause, the parents well might assert that they would not have consented to the testing procedure if they had not planned to act in the face of "positive" results. In addition, parents may claim that any reasonable person would reach the same result, and rely on the 1979 National Institutes of Health study that estimated that, of children found to be defective *in utero,* over 95 percent were aborted. Of course, by the time of the trial, the parents might be appreciably more negative towards the idea of raising a handicapped child than they would have been had they been informed of the genetic risk during pregnancy.[31] However, the cases indicate that parents have had no significant degree of difficulty in establishing that the mother would have aborted her handicapped unborn child.[32]

As we have seen, the act, duty, and causation elements in an action for wrongful life or wrongful birth are established rather easily. The real dispute in such claims arises over the question of damages. In a tort action, if there are no damages, or if they are incapable of measurement, then the plaintiff's case must fail. On this basis, courts generally have concluded that the wrongful life cause of action cannot be recognized because the damages that are claimed in that type of lawsuit cannot be measured, but that the wrongful birth cause of action can be recognized because the damages to the parents of a handicapped child are measurable.

In the 1967 case of *Gleitman v. Cosgrove,*[33] the New Jersey Supreme Court denied recovery for wrongful life, reasoning that it is impossible to measure the value of impaired life against no life at all. In that case, a blind and deaf infant sued his mother's doctors for negligently failing to inform the mother that prenatal rubella could cause defective offspring, thus denying her the opportunity to seek a eugenic abortion, which she alleged that she would have done. "The infant is therefore required to say not that he should have been born without defects but that he should not have been born at all,"[34] the court observed.

On the question of damages, the court noted that "the infant plaintiff would have us measure the difference between his life with defects against the utter void of nonexistence." It is "impossible to make such a determination," the court concluded, because the law "cannot weight the value of life with impairments against the nonexistence of life itself.... By asserting that he should not have been born, the infant makes it logically impossible for a court to measure his alleged damages because of the impossibility of making the comparison required by compensatory remedies."[35]

In *Berman v. Allan,*[36] the same court affirmed *Gleitman* in its denial of the child's wrongful life action. In *Berman,* the mother's doctor failed to inform her of the risk that she would give birth to a Down's syndrome (mongoloid) child and also neglected to advise her of the availability of the amniocentesis test. In rejecting the child's claim for damages, the *Berman* court said that the child, named Sharon, had not suffered any damage cognizable by the law from the fact of her birth. The court reasoned that one of the

most deeply held beliefs of our society is that life—whether experienced with or without a major handicap—is more precious than non-life.... Sharon, by virtue of her birth, will be able to love and be loved and to experience happiness and pleasure—emotions which are truly the essence of life and which are far more valuable than the suffering she may endure.... To rule otherwise would require us to disavow the basic assumption upon which our society is based.... (and) [t]his we cannot do.[37]

Curlender v. Bio-Science Laboratories,[38] decided in 1980 by a California Court of Appeals, marked a departure from the unanimous rejection by the courts of actions for wrongful life.[39] The California court recognized a wrongful life claim in the case of a girl born with Tay-Sachs disease and awarded economic damages. The court based its unprecedented decision on the maxim that there should be a legal remedy for every wrong committed.[40]

"The reality of the wrongful life concept," the court wrote, "is that . . . [the handicapped child] both exists and suffers, due to the negligence of others." The court added that "we need not be concerned with the fact that had the defendants not been negligent, [the child] . . . might not have come into existence at all, . . . [since] a reverent appreciation for life compels recognition that [the child] has come into existence with certain rights."[41] In asserting that the time had come to reject the *Gleitman* doctrine on the inascertainability of wrongful life damages, the *Curlender* court noted the "monumental implications" of the Supreme Court's historic abortion ruling in *Roe v. Wade* in legalizing the method by which defective births could be prevented.[42]

The *Curlender* court did not limit recovery under wrongful life to damages against the negligent physician, but raised the possibility that a child could sue his parents for having allowed him to be born alive with a handicap. Writing for the majority, Judge Bernard Jefferson argued that "If a case arose where, despite due care by the medical profession in transmitting the necessary warnings, the parents made a conscious choice to proceed with a pregnancy, with full knowledge that a seriously impaired infant would be born . . . we see no sound public policy that should protect those parents from being answerable for the pain, suffering and misery that they have wrought upon their offspring."[43] Underlying the court's wrongful life rationale is the assumption that was rejected by *Gleitman* and its progeny— that the child in a wrongful life suit is saying that she would be better off never having lived. By awarding damages to the child, the *Curlender* court not only involved itself in making the theretofore impossible judgment between the value of a "handicapped" life versus a "normal" one, but it implicitly asserted the rather radical proposition that in some cases life may be worse than no life.

A year later, the *Curlender* holdings were critiqued harshly by another district of the California Court of Appeals. In a similar wrongful life suit, *Turpin v. Sortini,*[44] the *Curlender* decision was said to have skirted the "fundamental problem of measuring damages, that is, comparing the value of impaired life against no life."[45] Casting its lot with the overwhelming majority of jurisdictions on the wrongful life question, the *Turpin* court observed that "Running through the cases is the central thought that in a wrongful life context the attempt to quantify the value of human life, whether or not afflicted with a defect, runs counter to the traditional notion of our American heritage which places a special value and premium on all human life, whether or not the physical or mental condition of the physical being which embodies that life is less than perfect."[46] In making its ruling, the *Turpin* court quoted the decisions of two other state courts. In *Becker v. Schwartz*,[47] the New York Court of Appeals argued that "There is no precedent for recognition ... of 'the fundamental right of a child to be born as a whole functional human being.' "[48] And in *Speck v. Finegold*,[49] a Pennsylvania court concurred. "Whether it is better to have never been born at all rather than to have been born with serious mental defects is a mystery which would lead us into the field of metaphysics, beyond the realm of our understanding or ability to solve."[50]

The *Turpin* court did not end its criticism of the *Curlender* ruling at the question of the award of wrongful life damages against physicians. It found its sister court mistaken on the idea of a defective child suing his parents as well. "The right of parents to make a decision to take the risk of having offspring with a defect rather than to live childless ... should not be tampered with by judicial intermeddling," the *Turpin* court declared.[51] The *Turpin* ruling also takes issue with the *Curlender* court's assertion that its decision was a logical extension of the Supreme Court's legalization of most abortions in *Roe v. Wade*. "There is nothing whatsoever in *Roe v. Wade*," said the *Turpin* court, "intimating that the *Wade* court had the intention of conferring a substantive right to sue theretofore nonexistent."[52]

Implicit in *Turpin* is the argument that far from being a logical extension of *Roe v. Wade,* the *Curlender* dicta regarding the child's right to sue his parents actually may be wholly inconsistent with *Roe*. The constitutional right to an abortion that was asserted in *Roe v. Wade* was grounded in a Fourteenth Amendment right to privacy, which the court previously had extended to marriage,[53] procreation,[54] contraception,[55] family relationships,[56] and childrearing.[57] This right protects independence and autonomy in the making of certain personal and familial decisions. A judicially imposed duty of parents to abort a defective child might well constitute impermissible state action abridging the mother's constitutional right to decide *not* to have an abortion.

While it remained for the California Supreme Court to resolve the conflict between its lower appellate courts on the wrongful life issue, *Turpin* helped to dilute the impact of *Curlender* as a portent of wider recognition for the tort of wrongful life.

In a May 1982 ruling, the California Supreme Court reconciled the dispute between the California Courts of Appeal decisions in the *Curlender* and *Turpin* cases by recognizing a limited "wrongful life" theory. In *Turpin v. Sortini*,[58] the court ruled that a child who is born with genetic defects may bring a "wrongful life" action against a physician who failed negligently to advise his parents of their genetic "risk." But the court added that damages must be limited to special damages for expenses of treating the genetic ailment.

The California court rejected the notion that any recognition of the "wrongful life" proper cause of action disavows society's respect for the inherent value of human life. But the court conceded that the impossibility of measuring the value of an impaired life against the value of no life at all makes an award of general damages impossible. In awarding special damages to the child, however, the court found no basis for distinguishing between the child's entitlement to damages for the special costs of his birth defect and those that are awarded to the parents in a typical "wrongful birth" action.

While wrongful life has been rejected by most courts, the wrongful birth concept is well entrenched and gaining strength. States recognizing wrongful birth include California, Michigan, Wisconsin, Texas, Ohio, Minnesota, New York, Pennsylvania, and New Jersey.[59] Wrongful birth has also been recognized for federal tort actions by the United States Court of Appeals for the Seventh Circuit.[60]

Several justifications for this trend, besides the availability of legal abortions, have been offered by the courts. A New Jersey opinion stated that disallowing the wrongful birth claim of a handicapped child's parents would ". . . immunize doctors from liability for inadequate genetic counselling."[61] A Texas court found it to be ". . . impossible to justify a policy that deprives the parents of information by which they could elect to terminate the pregnancy likely to produce the defective child, required that the pregnancy be continued until a defective child was born, and then denied the recovery from the (doctor) . . . of the costs of treating and caring for the defective child."[62] An Ohio court observed that constitutional law supported a public policy for the recognition of wrongful birth actions. The right to obtain an abortion is constitutionally guaranteed, it argued, and ". . . any attempt to limit damages would be an infringement of that right."[63]

Wrongful birth actions have enjoyed acceptance in the courts, while wrongful life lawsuits have not, because it generally is agreed that wrongful birth damages are measurable. Though some courts have said that these damages cannot be ascertained because the child is a blessing to the parents,[64] and that the value of the child cannot be valued in terms of money,[65] most jurisdictions have not sustained such reasoning. "The question is not the worth or sanctity of life," observed the Pennsylvania court in *Speck,* "but whether the doctors were negligent."[66]

In assessing wrongful birth damages, some courts have held that they should be limited restrictively to those that arise from the woman's pregnancy and the delivery of the child, including pain and suffering resulting from the pregnancy, related medical costs, and the loss of consortium during and immediately following the pregnancy.[67] Others allow recovery for any and all damages that are proximately caused by the negligence of the doctor. These include such categories as (1) expenses incurred during the pregnancy and delivery; (2) economic costs of rearing the child; (3) special expenses connected with a child's deformity; (4) the value of the woman's society, comfort, care, and protection that is lost to the other family members; (5) extra money needed to replenish the family budget so that the new arrival will not adversely affect the financial status of other family members; and (6) damages for mental and emotional distress.[68] Other courts do not permit recovery for emotional distress, because, they reason, that is one price that is paid for being a parent.[69] Some commentators have argued that the application of the benefits rule, which would discount damages by a measure of the value of the defective child to the parents, should be applied in order to offset any tendency to excessive awards.[70]

The progress of medical science in developing and improving the means of diagnosing birth defects in the womb doubtless will continue. Such tests will be made safer, easier, and cheaper. As the ability of medical science to treat some maladies of the fetus in the womb increases, the predominant use of the tests for "search and destroy" purposes will diminish commensurately. Thus, it is not unreasonable to predict that these factors, plus the proliferation of successful wrongful birth actions, will have the inescapable result of placing physicians under a legal duty to perform, or at least to recommend or to suggest, some type of prenatal defect diagnostic test during every pregnancy that comes under his care. As the wrongful birth concept gains acceptance, no doctor who values his economic security will be able to afford not to prescribe such evaluations.

This development would pose a difficult moral dilemma for doctors who oppose abortion as a matter of conscience. Since the current principal purpose of these procedures is to provide parents with information on whether their child might be handicapped so that, if she is, she may be aborted (provided there is no effective *in utero* treatment available), many physicians who are inclined to refuse to participate in abortion are not likely to involve themselves in the performance of such screening tests. If such tests do become a matter of routine, the right of doctors to object may be infringed and/or all such physicians in the area of obstetrics and gynecology may be forced by conscience to leave their chosen field of practice.

Numerous state legislatures have enacted statutes that insure that the rights of individuals who are opposed to abortion on a moral, religious, or ethical basis will not be abused in the post-*Roe* environment of permissiveness regarding abortion. The "individual conscience clause" type of statute typically provides that any medical practitioner who expresses a conscientious objection to abortion may not be required to participate in an abortion procedure.[71] *Roe*'s companion case, *Doe v. Bolton,* forms the basis of federal court doctrine in this area. In *Doe,* the U.S. Supreme Court noted its approval of a Georgia abortion law conscience clause.[72] Since *Doe,* the validity of an individual conscience clause never has been questioned seriously in the fedeal courts.[73] In addition, in 1973 Congress passed the

Church Amendment, which similarly protects individuals who conscientiously object to abortion from being compelled to participate in their performance.[74]

Professor Lynn Wardle of Brigham Young University has noted, "An individual's refusal, on moral grounds, to participate in performing an abortion is an exercise of conscience protected by the same right of privacy which now protects the woman's right to choose an abortion."[75] But does a doctor's right to object to participating in the performance of an abortion also extend to a right of refusal to disclose information about genetic risk to prospective parents? Would this foreclose their ability to obtain the information necessary to make an informed choice about abortion, which is a right that is protected by the *Roe* decision?

A commentator in the *Yale Law Journal* suggested that "it may be possible to avoid even this limited intrusion on the physician's . . . (ethical) convictions. . . . To serve legitimate needs of prospective parents, courts need not require objecting doctors either to undertake techniques to ascertain a person's genetic risk or even to provide prospective parents with genetic counseling." Instead, the comment suggests, "courts should require such physicians to conform to the standard of care exercised by other doctors in uncovering indications that prospective parents among their patients may be at genetic risk and to suggest that those parents go to other doctors to obtain any necessary additional testing and counseling. . . . Although this obligation may disturb the scruples of some practitioners, it is nevertheless needed to give prospective parents the opportunity to learn of their genetic risks."[76]

But for those genetic risks that lead to the discovery of a likely birth defect in the human fetus that cannot be treated *in utero,* and therefore may well lead to an abortion, the referral of the parents by a conscientious objector doctor to one who does not object may be the moral equivalent of participating in the actual performance of an abortion. By analogy, conscientious objectors to war are not required to refer their draft boards to a man who will fight even though the objector does not know for certain whether his referral will lead to the killing that he abhors. To do so might compromise or burden the protected right to object. Thus, it can be said logically that the creation of a legal duty for physicians to perform up to a given standard of care in the field of prenatal genetic diagnosis well may lead to serious interference with those doctors' protected rights to individual conscience.

It already has been noted how the recognition of the wrongful birth cause of action in tort law will contribute to the spread of prenatal genetic testing procedures until they become a part of the accepted notion of good medical practice in the field of pregnancy care. It is logical to extrapolate from that notion that more genetic testing would lead to the discovery of more fetal defects and that the discovery of more fetal defects would lead to a proliferation of genetically related abortions. An era of widespread eugenic abortions would have serious social implications.

Those few courts that have denied wrongful birth claims have asserted that allowing recovery would encourage a "Fascist-Orwellian societal attitude of genetic purity"[77] or the "Hitlerian elimination of the 'unfit.' "[78] Extension of the wrongful birth doctrine may manifest itself in increased intolerance for those handicapped persons who are already born. Yet, *Roe v. Wade* makes it clear that a woman may not be precluded from choosing to abort an offspring she had been planning to carry to term, if she is informed by prenatal testing of the likelihood of a birth defect.[79] Even during the final trimester, when the mother's right to an abortion is restricted to situations in which her life or health is endangered, the court's use of the term "health" is broad enough to encompass the emotional distress that the forthcoming birth of a defective child might entail.[80]

Thus, the rise of the wrongful birth suit may set in motion a chain of events that would result in the near total elimination of genetically defective births in the United States. This development would contravene the spirit of traditional social generosity toward the handicapped members of our society; furthermore, it would institutionalize and mandate a scheme of eugenics designed to eliminate, before birth, those who did not measure up to society's standards of "fitness."

After due consideration of the plausible implications and possible consequences of the establishment of wrongful birth and/or wrongful life in the theory of tort law, state legislatures may wish to abolish them as causes of action in the courts of their jurisdictions. This power, subject to any federal constitutional restrictions, is reserved to legislatures by state constitutions.

It may be argued that legislative abolition of the wrongful life tort causes of action would place a burden on the woman's constitutional right to choose to have an abortion. But the elimination of the causes of action would not ban the use of genetic screening tests by any means. Rather, it only would preclude physicians from having a "duty" to prescribe and/or to perform them. Hence, it would not burden even indirectly the abortion privacy right created by *Roe v. Wade*.

A proposed model statute reads as follows:

1. Wrongful Conception. There shall be no cause of action on behalf of any person, or by the parents or guardian of any person, that is based on a claim of that person that, but for an act or omission, he or she would not have been conceived and/or born.

2. Wrongful Birth. There shall be no cause of action on behalf of any person, or by the parents or guardian of such a person, that is based on a claim that, but for an act or omission, a human being, once conceived, would have been aborted.

3. Wrongful Life. There shall be no cause of action by any person against any other person or entity that is based on a claim that, but for an act or omission, he or she would have been aborted.

4. "Conception" means the fertilization of a human ovum by a human sperm, which shall be deemed to have occurred when the sperm has penetrated the cell membrane of the ovum.

5. For the purposes of this statute, a "human being" shall be deemed to exist from the point of conception.

Thus far we have discussed two developments of profound impact to the lives of handicapped and retarded individuals: (1) infanticide of newborns in the hospital ward through withdrawal of treatment and denial of nourishment, and (2) the use of prenatal screening for the purpose of performing a "eugenic" abortion and the rise of wrongful life and wrongful birth causes of action in the courts.

As we have seen, the law takes diametrically opposite positions on these two issues. On the one hand the law prescribes severe penalties for the practice of infanticide and on the other hand creates a situation where the incidence of abortion of handicapped preborn children could dramatically increase. It is doubtful, however, that this state of affairs will remain unchanged and the law continue to reflect such a contradictory position towards the handicapped unborn versus the handicapped newborn. The proliferation of wrongful birth actions and the widespread evidence of the practice of infanticide in American hospitals indicates that this contradiction could well be resolved by the adoption of a more permissive stance towards the practice of infanticide.

This development is not at all startling if one considers the logic behind eugenic abortion and wrongful birth/wrongful life lawsuits. The theory under which damages in such suits are awarded presupposes that there is such a thing as a life that is not worth living—in this case, the life of a handicapped or retarded person. The presumption that the life of an unborn child diagnosed as having a handicap will not be worth living (from the perspective of either the parents or the infant) will naturally lead society to question whether such life is worth protecting under the criminal law. The consequence of this thinking could be a laxity in the enforcement of homicide laws in cases involving the treatment of handicapped newborns. If we assume that the available evidence of the occurrence of infanticide is correct, it is apparent that such lax enforcement is becoming the rule rather than the exception. Continued entrenchment of this practice could well lead to the de facto decriminalization of almost all forms of infanticide of handicapped or otherwise "unfit" infants.

The growth of wrongful life and wrongful birth actions also may encourage infanticide in other ways. Consider the situation of the obstetrician, having cared for the mother throughout the term of pregnancy, who then delivers a child with birth defects. The possibility that, if the child should live, the parents might sue her for wrongful birth, or bring an action on behalf of the child for wrongful life, may act as a subtle pressure upon the physician in rendering advice on the treatment of the infant. This scenario clearly presents an ethical quandary to which the proper response would be a withdrawal of the physician from the case. However, as the concept of a "life not worth living" becomes an acceptable medico-legal doctrine, physicians may view infanticide as simply an alternative to eugenic abortions—and the law could support this view. In fact, the law regarding wrongful birth and wrongful life could evolve so as to hold physicians liable if they aggressively treat a handicapped newborn child whose life then becomes a "burden" to himself or his parents.

The consequence of these developments for the life and dignity of handicapped persons—and the values of our entire society—will be severe. Thus, even though the birth of a handicapped child inevitably poses burdens for parents and families, the treatment of such infants should not be considered a matter of purely private concern. If our society is serious in its commitment to the dignity of the handicapped, the law which condemns the killing of infants should be strengthened, and the encouragement of eugenic abortion by wrongful birth and wrongful life actions should be curtailed. If our law continues in its current direction, however, our profession of "rights" for the handicapped will be an empty one.

Notes

1. Monteleone & Moraczewski, *Medical and Ethical Aspects of the Prenatal Diagnosis of Genetic Disease,* in NEW PERSPECTIVES ON HUMAN ABORTION 41, 56 (T. Hilgers, D. Horan, & D. Mall eds. 1981).

2. Duff and Campbell, *Moral and Ethical Dilemmas in the Special-Care Nursery,* 289 NEW ENGLAND J. MED 890 (1973).

3. *Id.*

4. *See* Roe v. Wade, 410 U.S. 113, 154 (1973).

5. Duff and Campbell, *supra* note 2.

6. Jonsen et al., *Critical Issues in Newborn Intensive Care: A Conference Report and Policy Proposal,* 55 PEDIATRICS 756 (1975). *See generally,* Horan, *Euthanasia as a Form of Medical Management* in DEATH, DYING AND EUTHANASIA 196 (D. Horan & D. Mall eds. 1977).

7. Kamisar, *Some Non-Religious Views Against Proposed 'Mercy-Killing' Legislation,* 42 MINN. L. REV. 969 (1958).

8. Robertson, *Involuntary Euthanasia of Defective Newborns: A Legal Analysis,* 27 STAN. L. REV. 213 (1975).

9. *Id.*

10. For an excellent discussion of the very important distinction between active killing and letting one die a natural death, see Louisell, *Euthanasia and Biathanasia: On Dying and Killing,* 22 CATH. U. L. REV. 723 (1973).

11. Duff and Campbell, *supra* note 2, at 891.

12. *See* Gustafson, *Mongolism, Parental Desires and the Right to Life,* in PERSPECTIVES IN BIOLOGY AND MEDICINE, Summer 1973, at 529, 530.

13. Robertson, *supra* note 8.

14. *Id.* at 224-34.

15. *See* Horan, *Euthanasia, Medical Treatment and the Mongoloid Child: Death As A Treatment of Choice,* 27 BAYLOR L. REV. 76 (1975).

16. Horan, *supra* note 6, at 216.

17. *See* note 12, *supra.*

18. *See* Unpublished Address to Illinois Right to Life Committee, cited in Horan, *supra* note 6, at 220.

19. Jonas, *The Right to Die,* HASTINGS CENTER REPORT 31 (Aug. 1978).

20. *See, e.g.,* Robak v. United States, 658 F.2d 471 (7th Cir. 1981).

21. Most courts and commentators have spoken of a right of action of the parents of a defective child for wrongful life. This merits comment. Since the wrongful birth theory is predicated upon the right of abortion and since the constitutional right to an abortion that was enunciated by the U.S. Supreme Court in Roe v. Wade, 410 U.S. 113, 93 S.Ct. 705, 35 L. Ed.2d 147 (1973), vests in the pregnant woman only and not also in her husband and/or the father of the child, it is logical to conclude that it is the mother who has the cause of action for wrongful life. But all known wrongful birth cases have been brought by both parents, who together as a family suffer damages under the wrongful birth theory of recovery. A case might arise, however, where the father is dead, missing, or unknown. The mother then would sue alone, because she bears the burden of raising the child in question. Similarly, the mother of such a child might die, abandon the child to the father, or lose her to him in a custody action. In such a situation, the father alone could sue, though, if alive, but not in possession of the child, the mother might recover damages for emotional distress.

22. The National Institute of Child Health and Human Development (NICHD), National Registry for Amniocentesis Study Group, *Midtrimester Amniocentesis for Prenatal Diagnosis,* 236 J.A.M.A. 1471 (1976), at 1471.

23. Amniocentesis: the process in which a physician removes a sample of the amniotic fluid (which surrounds the fetus) between the fourteenth and sixteenth weeks of pregnancy. The amniotic fluid contains cells that are shed by the developing unborn child. Once these cells are cultured and tested, many disorders, including Down's syndrome (mongolism), can be detected. Sammons, *Ethical Issues in Genetic Intervention,* 23 SOC. WORK 237 (1978).

24. Ultrasonography utilizes sound waves, which are "bounced" off of the human fetus in the womb to read her shape and to detect any discernible abnormalities. *See* Monteleone & Moraczewski, *supra* at 47.

25. The alpha-fetoprotein (AFP) test is conducted between the sixteenth and the eighteenth weeks of pregnancy. Initially, it involves a blood test, which measures the AFP level in the blood of the mother, who receives amniotic fluid from her fetus into her circulation tract. If a high AFP level is found, an electronic ultrasound analysis is conducted. An amniocentesis test may result. National Center for Health Care Technology (NCHCT), *Maternal Serum Alpha-Fetoprotein: Issues in*

the Prenatal Screening and Diagnosis of Neural Tube Defects, Summary of Proceedings, July 1980, unpublished manuscript in the possession of the Americans United for Life, Chicago.

26. Note, *Mother and Father Know Best: Defining the Liability of Physicians for Inadequate Genetic Counseling,* 87 YALE L. J. 1488, 1494 (1978). [Hereinafter cited as YALE Note.]

27. There are more than sixty published decisions in which wrongful birth has been the theory of recovery. *See, e.g.,* Turpin v. Sortini, 174 Cal. Rptr. 128 (1981); Eisbrenner v. Stanley (Wisc. Ct. App. 1981); Gildiner v. Thomas Jefferson Univ. Hosp., 451 F.Supp. 692 (E.D. Pa. 1978); Berman v. Allan, 80 N.J. 421, 404 A.2d 8 (1979); Gleitman v. Cosgrove, 49 N.J. 22, 227 A.2d 689 (1967) *overruled in part by* Berman v. Allan, 80 N.J. 421, 404 A.2d 8 (1979); Becker v. Schwartz, 46 N.Y.2d 401, 386 N.E.2d 807, 413 N.Y.S.2d 895 (1978); Park v. Chessin, 88 Misc.2d 222, 387 N.Y.S.2d 204 (Sup. Ct. 1976), *modified and aff'd.,* 60 App. Div.2d 80, 400 N.Y.S. 110 (1977), *modified sub nom.* Becker v. Schwartz, 46 N.Y.2d 401, 386 N.E.2d 807, 413 N.Y.S.2d 895 (1978); Johnson v. Yeshiva Univ., 42 N.Y.2d 818, 364 N.E.2d 1340, 396 N.Y.S.2d 647 (1977); Howard v. Lecher, 42 N.Y.2d 109, 366 N.E.2d 64, 397 N.Y.S.2d 863 (1977); Karlsons v. Geuerinot, 57 App. Div.2d 73, 394 N.Y.S.2d 933 (1977); Stewart v. Long Island College Hosp., 58 Misc.2d 432, 296 N.Y.S.2d 41 (Sup. Ct. 1968), *modified,* 35 App. Div.2d 531, 313 N.Y.S.2d 502 (1970), *aff'd mem.,* 30 N.Y.2d 695, 283 N.E.2d 606, 322 N.Y.S.2d 640 (1972); Jacobs v. Theimer, 519 S.W.2d 846 (Tex. 1975); Dumer v. St. Michael's Hosp., 69 Wisc.2d 766, 233 N.W.2d 372 (1975). *See generally,* Comment, *Wrongful Birth: A Child of Tort Comes of Age,* 50 CIN. L. REV. 65 (1981).

28. This California court stands alone in recognizing the wrongful life proper theory. Curlender v. Bio-Science Laboratories, 106 Cal. App. 3d 811, 165 Cal. Rptr. 477 (1980), *writ of certiorari* to the California Supreme Court *denied.* The California court also recognized a right of a handicapped child to sue his parents for having let him be born. Both the wrongful life and right of a child to be born "whole" theories, however, were roundly criticized in a subsequent California Appeals Court decision. *See* Turpin v. Sortini, 174 Cal. Rptr. 128 (1981).

29. *See generally* D. LOUISELL AND H. WILLIAMS, MEDICAL MALPRACTICE 194–217 (1977), for a discussion of the duties incumbent upon physicians to maintain a professional standard of care and to keep abreast of new developments in fields of their specialty.

30. *See generally* Capron, *Informed Decision-Making in Genetic Counseling: A Dissent to the "Wrongful Life" Debate,* 48 IND. L. J. 581 (1973).

31. *See* YALE Note, *supra* note 26, at 1510 n.92.

32. *See* cases cited at note 27, *supra.*

33. 33 N.J. 22, 227 A.2d 689 (1967).

34. *Id.,* 227 A.2d at 692.

35. *Id.*

36. 80 N.J. 421, 404 A.2d 8 (1979).

37. *Id.,* 404 A.2d at 12–13.

38. 106 Cal. App. 3d 811, 165 Cal. Rptr. 477 (1980), *writ of certiorari* to Supreme Court of California *denied.*

39. *See, e.g.,* Park v. Chessin, 88 Misc.2d 222, 387 N.Y.S.2d 204 (Sup. Ct. 1976), *modified and aff'd,* 60 App. Div.2d 80, 400 N.Y.S.2d 110 (1977), *modified sub nom.* Becker v. Schwartz, 46 N.Y.2d 401, 386 N.E.2d 807, 413 N.Y.S.2d 895 (1978); Smith v. United States, 392 F.Supp. 654, 656 (N.D. Ohio 1975); Johnson v. Yeshiva University, 42 N.Y.2d 818, 364 N.E.2d 1340, 396 N.Y.S.2d 647 (1977); Greenberg v. Kliot, 47 App. Div.2d 765, 367 N.Y.S.2d 966 (1976).

40. 165 Cal. Rptr. at 489.

41. *Id.* at 488.

42. *Id.* at 487.

43. *Id.* at 488.

44. 174 Cal. Rptr. 128 (1981).

45. *Id.* at 131.

46. *Id.*

47. 46 N.Y.2d 401, 386 N.E.2d 807, 413 N.Y.S.2d 895 (1978).

48. *Id.* at 900.

49. 268 Pa. Super. 342, 408 A.2d 496 (1979).

50. 408 A.2d at 508.

51. 174 Cal. Rptr. at 133.

52. *Id.*

53. Loving v. Virginia, 388 U.S. 1, 12 (1967), as cited in Roe v. Wade, *supra,* at 152.

54. Skinner v. Oklahoma, 316 U.S. 535, 541–542 (1942) as cited in Roe v. Wade, *supra,* at 152.

55. Eisenstadt v. Baird, 405 U.S. 438 at 453–545 (1972); *Id.* at 460, 463–65 (White, J., concurring in result), as cited in Roe v. Wade, *supra,* at 152.

56. Prince v. Massachusetts, 321 U.S. 158, 166 (1944), as cited in Roe v. Wade, *supra,* at 153.

57. Pierce v. Soc'y of Sisters, 268 U.S. 510, 535 (1925), as cited in Roe v. Wade, *supra,* at 153.

58. 50 U.S.L.W. 2671 (Cal. 1982).

59. *See* Turpin v. Sortini, 174 Cal. Rptr. 128 (1981); Troppi v. Scarf, 31 Mich. App. 240, 187 N.W.2d 511 (1971); Dumer v. St. Michael's Hosp., 69 Wisc.2d 766, 233 N.W.2d 372 (1975); Jacobs v. Thermer, 519 S.W.2d 846 (Tex. 1975); Bowman v. Davis, 48 Ohio St.2d 41, 356 N.E.2d 496 (1976); Sherlock v. Stillwater Clinic, 260 N.W.2d 169 (Minn. 1977); Becker v. Schwartz, 46 N.Y.2d 40, 386 N.E.2d 807, 413 N.Y.S.2d 895 (1978); Berman v. Allen, 80 N.J. 421, 404 A.2d 8 (1979).

60. Robak v. United States, 658 F.2d 471 (7th Cir. 1981).

61. Berman v. Allen, 80 N.J. 421, 404 A.2d 8, 14 (1979).

62. Jacobs v. Thermer, 519 S.W.2d 846, 849 (Tex. 1975).

63. Bowman v. Davis, 48 Ohio St.2d 41, 356 N.E.2d 496, 499 (1976).

64. Shakeen v. Knight, 11 Pa. D. & C.2d 41, 45–46 (1957).

65. Terrell v. Garcia, 496 A.W.2d 124, 128 (Tex. Civ. App. 1973), *cert. denied,* 415 U.S. 927 (1974).

66. Speck v. Finegold, 408 A.2d 496, 503 (Pa. 1979).

67. Wilcynski v. Goodman, 73 Ill. App.3d at 63, 391 N.E.2d at 488; Bushman v. Burns Medical Center, 83 Mich. App. 453, 461, 268 N.W.2d 683, 686–87 (1978).

68. Bowman v. Davis, 356 N.E.2d at 497; *see* West v. Underwood, 132 N.J.L. 325, 326, 40 A.2d 610, 611 (1945); Ziemba v. Sternberg, 45 App. Div.2d at 231, 357 N.Y.S.2d at 267; as cited in Comment, *Wrongful Birth,* 50 CIN. L. REV. at 76 n. 86.

69. Speck v. Finegold, 408 A.2d 496, 503 (Pa. 1979).

70. *See, e.g.,* Comment, *Wrongful Birth,* 50 CIN. L. REV., *supra* note 68.

71. *See* L. WARDLE, THE ABORTION PRIVACY DOCTRINE 197 (1980).

72. Doe v. Bolton, 410 U.S. at 197, 198; as cited and analyzed in WARDLE, *supra* note 71, at 197–98.

73. WARDLE, *supra* note 71, at 198.

74. Health Programs Extension Act of 1973, Pub. L. No. 93-46, 87 Stat. 95 (1973) *as amended by* National Research Act, Pub. L. No. 93-348, 88 Stat. 353 (1974) (codified as 42 U.S.C. 300a-7, Supp. V. 1975); as cited in YALE Note, *supra* note 26, at 1510 n.94.

75. *See, generally.* L. TRIBE, AMERICAN CONSTITUTIONAL LAW (1978) §§ 14-10, at 856 (discussing conscientious objector rights); as cited in WARDLE, *supra* note 71, at 214 n.284.

76. YALE Note, *supra* note 26, at 1511–12.

77. *See* Gildiner v. Thomas Jefferson Univ. Hosp., *supra,* at 695. The court's majority rejected this theory.

78. *See* Dumer v. St. Michael's Hosp., 69 Wisc.2d at 780 (Hansen, J., dissenting).

79. Roe v. Wade, 410 U.S. 163 (1973).

80. *See, e.g.,* J. Ely, *The Wages of Crying Wolf: A Comment on Roe v. Wade,* 82 YALE L. J. 920, 921 (1973).

4
Treatment versus Nontreatment for the Handicapped Newborn

Eugene F. Diamond

Speaking as the official American witness at the Nuremberg doctors' trials, Dr. Leo Alexander commented on the genesis of the medical atrocities revealed during the proceedings. "Whatever proportions these crimes finally assumed, it became evident to all who investigated them that they had started from small beginnings. The beginnings at first were merely a subtle shift in emphasis in the basic attitudes of physicians. It started with the acceptance of the attitude, basic in the euthanasia movement, that there is such a thing as a life not worthy to be lived."[1] Today we can see the same shift in attitude occurring in American medicine. We can see the substitution of a "quality of life" ethic for a "sanctity of life" ethic and a discarding of our Hippocratic traditions in favor of the cost-benefit morality of the new technocracy.

Three recent events document and confirm this drift in medical ethics towards the acceptance of death as a treatment of choice—events that are liberally commented on by several other scholars in this volume. The first was the case of a mongoloid infant at Johns Hopkins University Medical Center, given notoriety by its dramatization in *Who Shall Survive?*, a film produced by the Kennedy Foundation.[2] The second milestone was the 1973 publication of *Moral and Ethical Dilemmas in the Special-Care Nursery* by Drs. Raymond Duff and A. G. M. Campbell.[3] This article chronicled the treatment of forty-three handicapped infants whose deaths were associated with the discontinuance or withdrawal of various forms of treatment. Some of these infants were born dying with untreatable maladies; some, however, were born with treatable conditions such as meningomyelocele and Down's syndrome with duodenal atresia who were denied treatment because of considerations of their prospective "quality of life."[4]

Eugene F. Diamond received his B.S. from University of Notre Dame and his M.D. from Loyola University. He is currently Professor of Pediatrics, Loyola University Stritch School of Medicine. He is Past President, Illinois Chapter of American Academy of Pediatrics, and is a member of the editorial boards of *Spina Bifida* and *Journal of Pediatric Social Work*.

The third milestone was the publication of proceedings of the Sonoma Conference on ethical issues in neonatal intensive care.[5] The twenty participants in this multidisciplinary conference included pediatricians, psychologists, social workers, professors of community medicine, medical economists, attorneys, and bioethicists. Among the questions asked of the panel was: "Would it ever be right to intervene directly to kill a self-sustaining infant?"[6] Two considerations about this question are crucial. First, to "intervene directly" indicates that what was at question was an act of positive killing, not passive euthanasia. Second, the question was directed at a "self-sustaining" infant—not one whose vital processes are maintained by a respirator or pacemaker. The response, given this understanding, was astounding: seventeen of the twenty conferees responded in the affirmative, two in the negative, and one individual was uncertain.[7] The shockwaves from Sonoma were widely felt, and Dr. Paul Ramsey has devoted a chapter in his *Ethics at the Edges of Life* to an analysis of this epoch-making conference.[8] It was as if a mirror had been held up to the various professions involved in neonatal care to reveal a Dorian Gray-like deterioration in ethics that we had not before sensed. Unwittingly, the medical profession had stepped onto the "slippery slope" in cases such as that documented in *Who Shall Survive?,* apparently failing to realize where this step might lead us.[9]

The consequences of introducing the "quality of life" ethic to treatment of the handicapped are better understood when a case such as that of the Johns Hopkins infant is more closely examined. The patient was a two-day-old, full-term male, a second-born to a married, middle-income Protestant couple in their twenties, parents of a normal two-year-old girl. The pregnancy was uneventful except for excess amniotic fluid accumulation and delivery was normal. Greenish vomiting began shortly after birth and there was slight abdominal distension and moderate dehydration, but no evidence of cardiac abnormalities. The infant had mongoloid facies and features and on X-ray of the abdomen showed intestinal obstruction. The clinical impression was Down's syndrome and duodenal atresia.

After discussion with the parents, a decision was made not to operate to repair the obstruction due to the duodenal atresia. All feeding and fluids were withheld and the child eventually died, after fifteen days, from starvation and dehydration.[10]

It is important to examine the rationalization involved in such medical management in order to understand the implication of this new development in medical ethics and its significance for the profession and the society as a whole. The rationale is not easy to understand and a short ten years ago would have been considered monstrous and unacceptable. Perhaps we can begin to understand if we break the elements of the physical problem down. Suppose first that the infant in question had neither Down's syndrome nor duodenal atresia. Obviously, the physician could not kill the child and nursery personnel could not fail to nourish him or her. Our law makes it clear that the parents' dominion over children does not extend to wilful acts or negligence which will harm the child.[11] No exception to this rule is made in the event that a child is born with a handicap.[12] In the case of a child born with Down's syndrome but without duodenal atresia, most would agree that medical personnel would certainly be obligated to nourish and treat the child. Indeed, if nurses or physicians were to concur in a decision of the parents not to feed such a child, they would be guilty of active participation in a killing act and not just an omission.[13]

Now suppose that the child was born normal except for duodenal atresia. This defect can be corrected by an operative procedure with an approximate survival rate of 98 percent. The pediatrician cannot fail to recommend an operation in such circumstances, nor can a surgeon fail to operate. Parents who refuse to consent to such an operation would almost certainly be compelled to do so by legal action.[14]

Finally, consider the case of the "Johns Hopkins" baby: born with both Down's syndrome and duodenal atresia. Here, for some reason, there is a change in the rules and apparently in a physician's duty as well. The physician's duty obviously derives from the physician-patient relationship. Traditional medical ethics has obviously had exquisite difficulty in making a distinction between one's duty to a retarded child and one's duty to a normal child. It has held, if anything, that there was a greater obligation to the retarded. Thus, if I have the obligation to care for a child without Down's syndrome, how can I avoid my obligation to the child with Down's syndrome? And if I have a clear obligation to care for the child with Down's syndrome, does not that obligation compel me to perform a duty which I am physically capable of performing? In this case, am I not obligated to perform a virtually risk-free operation? These would seem like rhetorical questions expecting the answer "yes," and yet, I do not hear a strong affirmative reply from my profession and I wonder why. Is it because of a judgment that I have passed on the child with Down's syndrome that places him in an isolated, unheard position as he tries to incur my obligation to him? If so, I should then ask, Who is this mongoloid child and by what authority may I treat him as if he does not have the rights of other children?

Children with Down's syndrome do far better at home and only a small percentage should ever be institutionalized. Most of these children should not be placed away from home—and will not be if the pediatrician and obstetrician perform properly. The Down's syndrome child who has broken his mother's heart will usually mend it again in two or three years.

There is no avoiding, of course, the initial reaction of grief. The parents should be allowed active grief without detachment. They should, however, recognize the baby as their own and should have physical contact with it. One of the recurrent mistakes made is that of the obstetrician who says, "Don't take him home or you will become attached to him." First of all, becoming attached to your own child is not necessarily a bad development. Secondly, this attachment does not begin with taking the baby home. The mother has already been "attached" to this baby for nine months. He was a presence within her from the earliest weeks and a more profound and intimate presence as he began to move, to grow, to accompany her to bed, to go literally everywhere with her.

If parents see the physician treat the Down's child as he would any other child, they draw their strength from him. One disadvantage for the physician is that the descriptive terminology used in describing the features of the child with Down's syndrome is often pejorative. Such children are described as having a "Simian" foot or a "Simian" crease, a "Mongoloid" facies, a "saddle" nose, a "spade" hand and so on. When the doctor describes her baby in terms usually reserved for foreigners or monkeys, it is not surprising that the mother will hesitate to welcome it into her home.

When we examine the handicapped child under the law it is clear that there is no legal authority to support this derogation of rights of the handicapped or retarded. If there was ever a doubt that the retarded have rights, those doubts have been categorically removed. Article II of the United Nations Draft Convention on the Rights of the Child, to be presented to the U.. General Assembly in 1982, states that the "Parties to the present Convention recognize the right of a mentally or physically disabled child to special protection and care ... and shall extend appropriate assistance to such a child. A disabled child shall grow up and receive education in conditions designed to achieve his fullest possible social integration."[15] Over the past two decades, the federal courts in the United States have responded to the nontreatment and abuse of handicapped and retarded persons in state hospitals. In the 1965 St. Elizabeth's hospital case in Washington, D.C., it was ruled that "the Retarded must be cared for and trained, not just kept in custody." This standard was also applied in the Pennhurst case in Pennsylvania in 1972. In an Alabama case, a federal court held that these rights "are present ones and must not only be declared but secured at the earliest practicable time."[16] It is inconsistent with the holdings in these cases for a physician to deny treatment—to the extent of withholding *food* and *water*—to an infant because of his or her handicapped condition.

How is it possible, then, that these rights have been violated and abridged in this case? What are the factors that have conditioned public acceptance of the fact that medical personnel chose to starve this baby to death rather than to go to court to compel restorative surgery? The most important factor, in my opinion, has been the development of large amniocentesis programs funded by the March of Dimes or by federal agencies. The development of these programs and the acceptance of abortion as a means to "prevent" the occurrence of handicaps such as Down's syndrome has led to the creation of a "free fire zone" during which mongoloid children may be killed by abortion during the late-middle and last trimester. There are no restrictions on aborting Down's syndrome children even after viability. Such a practice naturally leads to the possibility of abandoning such infants if they survive prenatal screening and are born alive. Recently a pediatric journal published an article entitled "The Prevention of Mongolism through Amniocentesis." I wrote a letter to the editor pointing out that the only way to prevent mongolism was at conception by preventing the fertilization of a 24-chromosome gamete by a 23-chromosome gamete, or better yet by preventing nondisjunction during meiosis. Aborting a child with Down's syndrome only prevents his birth. The editor refused to publish the letter, calling me a "religious fanatic." Presumably he was referring to genetics as a religion, which it well may become.

Just as the sacrifice of newborn infants with Down's syndrome is the logical extension of the abortion of viable infants with Down's syndrome, the rationalization of withholding care for newborns establishes the precedent for neglecting older children with Down's syndrome. In the early 1970s, Congressman Walter Sackett of the Florida legislature, a physician, introduced a "Death With Dignity" bill, ostensibly aimed at allowing individuals to execute a "living will."[17] Congressman Sackett, however, in his testimony before Senator Church's Special Committee on the Aging in 1973, betrayed an underlying motive in proposing his bill. This motive was to promote what he described as "a major change in American law." He disclosed that the "first step" of allowing individuals to execute their own living will was to be followed by a "second step" of allowing next of kin to execute living wills on behalf of individuals and a "third step" of allowing physicians to execute the living will when next of kin were not available. He suggested that as many as 90 percent of institutionalized mental defectives in Florida might qualify for elimination under the provisions of steps two and three. Sackett also proposed that the retarded be evaluated by the criteria of cost-benefit analysis. "Now where is the benefit," he asked, "in these 1,500 severely retarded, who never had a rational thought?" Such patients, he stated, should be allowed to die by withdrawing all medical treatment; for example, by not treating adolescents with Down's syndrome if they contract pneumonia.[18]

Sackett's proposals are not an isolated phenomenon, but rather represent the encroachment of cost-benefit analysis upon traditional medical doctrine. This intrusion of government economists into medical care and planning has in my opinion been an important factor affecting society's attitudes towards treatment of the handicapped. Jonathan Swift describes the Lilliputians as believing that Gulliver's watch was his god because he consulted it before making important decisions. In the American technocracy the computer has become this kind of god. Predictably, in a land of conspicuous consumption, computer technology has reached its zenith in the area of marketing and finance. Most billing is done by computer and the computer always has the instant answer to the great American question, "How much will it cost?" No important decision is made without a cost-benefit analysis and what used to be called basic verities are now rejected on the scales of economy.

A recurring theme in medicine today, consequently, is the notion of the "finite health dollar." We are told that, if we could only divert the money spent on the custodial care of retarded children into research or nutrition, we would soon have cures for these afflictions and many other social ills as well.[19] What proponents of this line of thinking obscure is the fact that caring for retarded children, and funding research to prevent future handicaps, are not mutually exclusive. Who can say that in a $2 trillion economy we cannot achieve both goals by shifting our priorities? Given the relatively slight cost of the needed care and research, we can probably do whatever we set our minds to do in this realm.

Yet if we set our minds in another direction, the consequences for our medical profession and our society will be tragic. Our preoccupation with materialism and our consequent acceptance of death as a treatment of choice threatens the integrity of the medical profession as one devoted to healing. We should have realized this earlier, because of the horror brought on by another society of recent unhappy memory that employed violence as a weapon in its pursuit of "order" and "perfection." In that society efficiency and bloodletting were caught up in the vortex of the Holocaust. In the vanguard of the Holocaust were those who wore a caduceus alongside their swastikas and who provided the expertise, even the genius, for the implementation of final solutions.

A third important factor that has led to our shifting attitudes on the treatment of handicapped infants has been the attempt to substitute the "quality of life ethic" for the "sanctity of life" ethic in medicine. Applying this ethic to the child with Down's syndrome and duodenal atresia, we need only declare that life is not worth living unless it can be lived without handicaps. From this cult of perfection, then, we derive a new definition of death. Death becomes living with handicaps. To repair the duodenal atresia would only prolong the "living death" of Down's syndrome.

It is possible that this alleged compassion for the handicapped may be entirely misplaced. There is no evidence that the handicapped child would rather not go on living. As a matter of fact, handicapped persons commit suicide far less often than normal persons. An interesting study was done at the Anna Stift in Hanover, Germany, a center where a large number of children with phocomelia, due to thalidomide, are cared for. Psychological testing on these children indicated that they indeed value their lives, that they are glad that they were born and that they look forward to the future with hope and pleasant anticipation.[20]

We are listening to the wrong experts. Mass screening programs to detect genetic defects, the intrusion of the cost-benefit approach to treatment decisions, and adherence to the quality-of-life ethic have all promoted infanticide in America. I have, however, taken my own poll on the Johns Hopkins case and have come up with some interesting statistics. When left with the choice between surgery and starvation, the parents, grandparents, and siblings of children with Down's syndrome vote overwhelmingly for surgery as do pediatricians who subspecialize in the care of the retarded. Nurses and other primary physicians cast a majority vote for surgery and only surgeons and educators are unsure. (One surgeon described the withholding of food and water for two weeks as "conservative management.")

This journey, above and beyond its cost in human life, may destroy the status of physicians as a trusted, learned profession. Every time we let something like the Johns Hopkins case happen, we all lose something. What we lose is a little of what sustains us, a little of what holds us together. We become more as technocrats, less of a learned profession. If a physician becomes preoccupied with the social and public good, who will protect the individual rights of the patient?

Consider the case of the nurse in Decatur, Illinois, who had to conceal water on her person when she visited a mongoloid infant suffering in his twelfth day without nourishment. The water was merely to moisten the baby's eyes so that he could, at least, close his dessicated eyelids. To her, no doctor will have status again.

We continually try to convince ourselves that this new ethic of death is demanded by the difficulty of caring for the handicapped infant. Seldom stated, however, is the fact that there are fewer handicapped children being born as a result of improved prenatal care, viral vaccines, and the control of drugs given to pregnant women—or that infinitely more can be done to rehabilitate handicapped children than we could a generation ago or even a decade ago or even five years ago. "Our success has been our undoing," we tell one another with perverted logic. We are convinced that when we could do nothing for any child, there were no agonizing decisions. How simple it was to talk to parents of children with meningomyelocele in the 1940s. Shunts and other surgical methods being unknown, there was little other alternative to committing such children to institutions. There, shielded from the eyes of the public and most of the medical profession, the answers came automatically. Little heads blew up like watermelons and tiny increments of pressure finally built up to a point where they turned off vital centers. Enteric organisms poured out of incontinent sphincters into ruptured meningeal sacs and there were very few drugs to control the infections.

Theoretically, it is probably true that we should not sustain a life that is totally without any potential for human experience or relating, at least not by extraordinary means. Two questions arise in the application of this standard. First of all, do we really mean that there is no person who can relate to the human being in question? Second, does the agency that applies that standard—parent, physician, committee—have sufficient expertise to accurately relate the defective person to the norm or standard for withholding life support? These are extremely important questions. The psychological profile of persons present when the defective infant is born will differ greatly from that of the caretakers who would be expected to assume long-term responsibility for follow-up care. Acute-disease hospitals and their personnel, especially in intensive-care units, are accustomed to instant gratification in applying therapeutic modalities. Dramatic corrective surgery, resuscitative brinksmanship, and rapid turnover of patients are their daily expectation. They are inclined to have a low frustration tolerance and to doubt the validity of large investments of professional time and energy to realize small returns of stable or slightly altered function. Those whose daily life involves the care of mentally retarded or other chronically handicapped children, however, are a different breed altogether.

For ten years I visited at the Misericordia Home in Chicago, usually with a contingent of medical students. Severely retarded and pathetically handicapped children populated this institution along with a larger, less-retarded group of mongoloid children. Each child, ambulatory or not, was fully dressed, including shoes and stockings, each morning. The institution was immaculate. Someone in the institution was capable of relating closely to every child, and, as we made rounds, at every bedside there would be a staff member, usually an aide or a nurse, who could tell us the child's history. Severe hydrocephalics and markedly obtunded, neurologically damaged children were called by name and regarded as individuals. Their needs were appreciated and even anticipated. Their disease-related irascibility was understood, explained away, and assuaged by acts of comfort.

Almost all the students came away with the impression that something very human, and medically dramatic, was happening in that institution. Certainly, there are those unfortunate patients who in the act of dying cannot escape from measures that merely prolong their death. To withdraw treatment from such a patient is quite different from suggesting that someone not now dying can be judged as having a quality of life that precludes their ever relating to another human being at a meaningful level. If there are persons in this latter category, who truly cannot relate to another human being, they are few and far between. To use them as a paradigm for the withholding of medical care as an ordinary option is so susceptible to misinterpretation as to be dangerous and counterproductive. In fact, all attempts to circumscribe and isolate examples of "quality of life" criteria for sustaining medical care seem to reemphasize the superior workability of the traditional "sanctity of life" criteria for medical decision making. If one stands at the bedside or the cribside convinced of the irreducible value of every human person, he is, in the practical order, much better equipped to make rational and humane decisions in his patient's best interests.

Protests on behalf of "parents' rights" in the making of lethal decisions affecting their newborn children are particularly inappropriate when one knows the circumstances under which such decisions are usually made. What parent is really free in making such a decision? Deeply in mourning for the perfect child she planned on, who is now irretrievably lost, the mother faces a phalanx of professionals who are usually strangers in an unfamiliar, stainless, even hostile hospital environment. Her husband usually defers to her wishes, and her wishes are usually determined by the way the circumstances are presented. If the need for immediate care is separated, as it should be, from the long-term prognostic implications of survival, she will usually opt for that care. She should not be isolated from the knowledge that the society will accept its appropriate legal obligation to share the long-term burden in most instances.

While it is true that ordinary and extraordinary means are relative and dependent on circumstance, it is also true that what is ordinary for an affluent, intelligent child cannot be extraordinary for a poor, retarded child. If a low-risk operation for intestinal obstruction is indicated in an otherwise normal child, it is indicated in a mongoloid child. If a shunt is indicated for the only child of affluent professionals, it is also indicated for the comparably handicapped child born to welfare parents with other normal children. The defective child who will enter a loving home deserves no more from his physician than the defective child who will enter a deprived or broken home.

The importance of maintaining the highest regard for the sanctity of life can only really be appreciated in the context of the kind of society in which we live. The dominating realities of the American system as they are brought to bear upon the weak, the handicapped, and the dispossessed have very little to do with the recent explosion of scientific knowledge. The real jeopardy posed by the last quarter of the twentieth century is not that we will ignore technological advancement and cling to the obsolete. Rather, it is that this society has become committed to violence as a solution to problems posed by economic considerations. With a birthrate below replacement and with the mean age of the population constantly increasing, the next focus will unquestionably be upon the "quality of life" of the aged. The official position of our federal government condones violent death for sacred unborn life throughout pregnancy. Not content with killing the fetus, the medical profession has proposed to perform nonbeneficial research assaults on him in anticipation of his demise.

If we are to reclaim protection for the unborn child, we cannot concede the logical extension of the abortion mentality into the nursery. The sanctity-of-life ethic which now spreads its tattered mantle of protection over newborn defective infants must be upheld. It is really protecting all of us.

Notes

1. Alexander, *Medical Science Under Dictatorship*, 241 NEW ENGLAND J. MED. 39, 44 (1949).

2. JOSEPH P. KENNEDY FOUNDATION, REPORT OF THE JOSEPH P. KENNEDY FOUNDATION INT'L SYMPOSIUM ON HUMAN RIGHTS, RETARDATION AND RESEARCH, Oct. 16, 1971 [hereinafter cited as KENNEDY FOUNDATION REPORT].

3. 289 NEW ENGLAND J. MED. 890 (1973).

4. *Id.* at 890–91.

5. *See* ETHICS OF NEWBORN INTENSIVE CARE (A. Jonsen & M. Garland eds. 1976); Jonsen et al., *Critical Issues in Newborn Intensive Care: A Conference Report and Policy Proposal,* 55 PEDIATRICS 756 (1975).

6. *Id.*

7. *Id.*

8. P. RAMSEY, ETHICS AT THE EDGES OF LIFE 228–67 (1978).

9. The "slippery slope" concept is analogous to the "wedge" principle described by, among others, Dr. Norman St. John-Stevas and Yale Kamisar. *See* ST. JOHN-STEVAS, DEATH, DYING AND THE LAW (1964), and Kamisar, *Some Non-Religious Views Against Proposed Mercy-Killing Legislation,* 42 MINN. L. REV. 969 (1958). In this matter, the "slippery slope" argument claims that the first step of "benign neglect" towards the infant with multiple, but treatable, abnormalities, in and of itself an erroneous decision, will lead to acceptance of even greater horrors, such as the direct killing of infants. *See also* Alexander, *supra,* note 1.

10. KENNEDY FOUNDATION REPORT, *supra,* note 2.

11. *See* Horan, *Euthanasia as Medical Management,* in DEATH, DYING AND EUTHANASIA 196, 219 (D. Horan & D. Mall eds. 1980).

12. Robertson, *Involuntary Euthanasia of Defective Newborns: A Legal Analysis,* 27 STAN. L. REV. 213, 218–24 (1975).

13. *Id.* at 225–26.

14. Horan, *supra,* note 11 at 217.

15. Draft Convention on the Rights of the Child, 7 Oct. 1981. Copy on file with editors.

16. *See* Rouse v. Cameron, 373 F.2d 451 (D.C. Cir. 1966); Wyatt v. Aderholt, 503 F.2d 1305 (5th Cir. 1974), *aff'g* Wyatt v. Stickney, 325 F.Supp. 781 (M.D. Ala. 1971); Wyatt v. Stickney, 344 F.Supp. 387 (M.D. Ala. 1972); *aff'd in relevant part sub. nom* Wyatt v. Aderholt, 503 F.2d 1305 (5th Cir., 1974); Halderman v. Pennhurst State School & Hosp., 612 F.2d 84 (35d Cir. 1979).

17. *See* discussion in Diamond, *The Deformed Child's Right to Life,* in DEATH, DYING AND EUTHANASIA 127, 131–33 (D. Horan & D. Mall eds. 1980).

18. U.S. SENATE HEARINGS, 92nd Cong., v. 1, Special Committee on Aging, *Death With Dignity: An Inquiry Into Related Public Issues* (Testimony of Walter Sackett, M.D.).

19. *Id.* at 30.

20. Hauberg, *Symposium on Current Abortion Law,* 137 ILL. MED. J. 678 (1967).

5
Modern Achievements in the Intact Salvage of Very Small Premature Infants

Craig L. Anderson

Let me ask my fellow laborers in our beloved profession, in the interest of our own honor and usefulness; in the interest of the dear children we are called upon to administer unto, and in the interest of the anxious and earnest students seeking to know the geography of the whole field of medicine—I say in the interest of all these, let us endeavor to appreciate and teach the true relation existing between the child and the adult; the sprout and the full-grown tree, and forever divorce this branch of our practice from the unnatural relation heretofore forcibly maintained between it and gynecology and obstetrics. And let us wake up to the realization of the fact that there is more real science in the proper practice of medicine among the children, . . . and also that the treatment of children calls for the best efforts of the most scientific and skillful of our ranks, and that any indifference to or inclination to shift responsibility of their treatment, is only an evidence of our weakness in this direction, and our nonappreciation of and unwillingness to perform our whole duty.

So wrote Dr. J. B. Casebeer in the first volume of the *Journal of the American Medical Association* in 1883.[1]

Since Casebeer's century-old appeal to the medical profession for consideration of children's illness as separate and distinct from the adult, we have witnessed, particularly in the last twenty-five years, remarkable scientific achievements in the understanding and care of the newborn. Questions are now being raised about the economic costs, long-term medical outcome, and wisdom of resuscitating the very low birth weight infant.[2] It is the purpose of this short chapter to consider the current status of these very important issues.

Craig L. Anderson received his B.S. and M.D. from the University of Wisconsin, Madison. He is currently Assistant Professor of Pediatrics and Obstetrics/Gynecology, Loyola University Stritch School of Medicine, and Director, Newborn Intensive Care Unit, Loyola University Medical Center, Maywood, Illinois.

Neonatal mortality rates have been significantly reduced in the United States particularly over the past fifteen years. Lee et al.,[3] using birth-weight-specific neonatal mortality rates, calculated an overall mortality rate of twenty live births per thousand in 1950, contrasted to twelve live births per thousand in 1975. The most rapid decline has occurred since 1965 in spite of the fact that there was a rise in the rate of very low birth weight infants (those weighing less than 1,500 grams). This improvement coincides with major changes in perinatal medical care in the United States. Technological advances and the establishment of regional intensive care units are the important factors contributing to improved survival rates. Graven et al.[4] demonstrated a reduction in neonatal mortality of nearly 40 percent among Wisconsin perinatal-center affiliated hospitals in contrast to 26 percent for unaffiliated hospitals during the period 1966 to 1972.

In 1979 10 percent of infants weighing less than 2,500 grams died in our institution. Nearly half of these deaths occurred in infants weighing less than 1,000 grams. Although infants weighing less than 1,000 grams have the highest mortality, improving survival rates in this weight group have been noted by Wung et al.,[5] Hach et al.,[6] and our own experience where 47 percent survived in 1979. Improvement has also been noted among infants with hyaline membrane disease as reported by Tooley.[7] He observed survival rates in excess of 75 percent among infants weighing more than 1,501 grams at birth in 1977–78 compared to 50 percent during 1965–66.

As noted above, medical care has contributed to an improvement in neonatal survival, yet there are other important factors influencing premature birth that are identifiable prior to delivery. Adequacy of prenatal care is one of these factors. Illinois Department of Public Health Statistics for 1976 reveal a neonatal mortality rate of 3.8 for those mothers receiving adequate prenatal care contrasted to 15.2 for those with inadequate or unknown prenatal care.[8] Similarly, if mother's parity was two or more with no living children, the neonatal mortality was 25.3 compared to 10.8 for those of parity one. Maternal age is also an important factor. There were 1,360 mothers aged fifteen to nineteen years of parity three with a neonatal mortality rate of 47.8, contrasted to 19.4 with parity one.

The incidence of major handicaps among low birth weight infants has continued to fall. Lubchenco[9] reported major handicaps in 100 percent of infants weighing less than 1,000 grams born during the period 1947 to 1950. This contrasts sharply with the 7 percent incidence reported by Reynolds[10] for the same birth weight delivered between 1966 and 1975. Pape et al.[11] have published extensively on the follow-up of the low birth weight infant. Their data are revealing in that all of the infants were delivered at outlying hospitals and then transferred for neonatal intensive care. Of infants born in 1974 and followed to age two years, 9 percent had a major neurologic deficit and 21 percent had severe developmental delay. Kumar et al.[12] recently reported a 14 percent incidence in developmental delay for a similar population except that all were born at a perinatal center.

Currently, the most difficult birth weight group to care for is the infant group weighing between 500 and 800 grams. This group poses major ethical dilemmas in terms of providing and maintaining life support systems. Fitzhardinge et al.[13] recently reported a 20 percent survival rate in this weight group with 15 percent having major neurologic handicaps and 48 percent with mean Bayley scores less than 85. If the infant's birth weight was less than 700 grams, none were normal at eighteen months and only 2 percent were normal if gestational age (age of child *in utero*) was less than twenty-six weeks.

McCarthy et al.[14] reported mean hospitalization cost by birth weight among infants cared for in Denver, Colorado. If birth weight was between 500 and 999 grams, mean charge for survivors was $25,157. This contrasted sharply with those weighing between 2,000 and 2,499 grams where mean cost was $5,414. Anderson et al.[15] recently reported a mean hospitalization cost of $10,557 in Chicago for surviving infants less than thirty-four weeks gestation if the child was delivered in a perinatal center, compared to $18,729 for the infant born at an outlying hospital and transferred for neonatal intensive care.

* * *

Neonatal mortality and morbidity has continued to decline for all low birth weight infants with the exception of babies weighing less than 800 grams. The ethical issues raised regarding providing and maintaining life support systems for this later group could well have been raised thirty years ago for infants weighing between 1,250 and 1,500 grams; yet, with the improved medical care available today, the outlook is quite good for these larger low birth weight infants. As Casebeer suggested long ago, "the best efforts of the most scientific and skillful of our ranks" will be required to further improve the intact survival of very small premature infants.

Notes

1. Casebeer, *Pediatric Medicine and its Relation to General Medicine,* 1 J.A.M.A. 327 (1883).

2. Jonsen, Phibbs, Tooley, & Garland, *Critical Issues in Newborn Intensive Care: A Conference Report and Policy Proposal,* 55 PEDIATRICS 756 (1975).

3. Lee, Paneth, Gartner, Pearlman, & Gruss, *Neonatal Mortality: An Analysis of Recent Improvement in the United States,* 70 AM. J. PUB. HEALTH 15 (1980).

4. S. GRAVEN & H. CALLON, WISCONSIN STATE DIVISION OF HEALTH REPORT (1976).

5. Wung, Koons, Driscoll, & James, *Changing Incidence of Bronchopulmonary Dysplasia,* 95 J. PEDIATRICS 845 (1979).

6. Hack, Fanaroff, & Merkatz, *The Low Birth Weight Infant—Evolution of a Changing Outlook,* 301 NEW ENGLAND J. MED. 1162 (1979).

7. Tooley, *Epidemiology of Bronchopulmonary Dysplasia,* 95 J. PEDIATRICS 851 (1979).

8. STATE OF ILLINOIS DEPARTMENT OF PUBLIC HEALTH, ANNUAL SUMMARY OF SELECTED ACTIVITIES IN HOSPITAL MATERNITY SERVICES (1976).

9. Lubchenco, Horner, Reed, et al., *Sequelae of Premature Birth,* 106 AM. J. DISEASES CHILDREN 101 (1963).

10. Reynolds & Taghizadeh, *Improved Prognosis of Infants Mechanically Ventilated,* 52 ARCHIVES DISEASE IN CHILDHOOD 97 (1977).

11. Pape, Buncie, Ashby, & Fitzhardinge, *The Status at Two Years of Low Birth Weight Infants Born in 1974 with Birth Weights of Less Than 1001 Grams,* 92 J. PEDIATRICS 253 (1978).

12. Kumar, Anday, Sachs, Ting, & Delivaria-Papadopoulous, *Follow Up Studies of Very Low Birth Weight Infants (1250 Grams) Born and Treated Within a Perinatal Center,* 66 PEDIATRICS 438 (1980).

13. Fitzhardinge & Bennett-Britton, *Is Intensive Care Justified for Infants Less Than 801 Grams at Birth?,* 14 PEDIATRICS RESEARCH, 590 (1980) (abstract).

14. McCarthy, Koops, Honeyfield, & Butterfield, *Who Pays the Bill for Neonatal Intensive Care?,* 95 J. PEDIATRICS 755 (1979).

15. Anderson, Aladjem, Ayuste, Caldwell, & Ismail, *An Analysis of Maternal Transport within a Suburban Metropolitan Region,* 140 AM. J. OBSTETRICS & GYNECOLOGY 499 (1981).

6

Treatment Choices
for the Infant
with Meningomyelocele

James T. Brown and David G. McLone

From prehistoric art forms we know that meningomyelocele was known to ancient peoples. Plato and Aristotle advocated infanticide in such cases, and it is well known that the Spartans put this into practice. The first attempt at surgical closure of a meningomyelocele lesion occurred in the seventeenth century—with expectedly poor results.[1] Until about twenty to thirty years ago, infants with meningomyelocele were essentially untreatable because there was no effective therapy for the lesion and its associated problems, such as hydrocephalus. However, with the development of extracranial cerebrospinal fluid diversionary procedures—that is, shunts—for hydrocephalus,[2] along with advances in anesthesia, neonatology, and antibiotic therapy, in the early 1950s it became possible to treat this condition with improved survival. Indeed, the first call for aggressive treatment of such children came in the early 1960s from England.[3]

It is still uncertain why this congenital anomaly occurs. We know that late in the third week of gestation the primitive neural plate begins to infold to form a neural tube, which is the forerunner of the spinal cord. For a short time in the development of the neural tube there is an opening, called the posterior neuropore. It is here that the anomaly seems to occur. There are two theories as to why.[4] The first is that the posterior neuropore fails to obliterate normally. The second theory is that the neuropore does close normally, but later in development ruptures open, resulting in the meningomyelocele anomaly.

James T. Brown received his B.S. from Marquette University and his M.D. and M.S. (surgery) from Northwestern University. He is currently Associate in Surgery at Northwestern University Medical School, and Attending Surgeon (neurosurgery) at Children's Memorial Hospital, Chicago.

David G. McLone received his B.S. in chemistry from Michigan State University, his M.D. from the University of Michigan, and his Ph.D. in neuroanatomy from Northwestern University. He is currently Chairman of Pediatric Neurosurgery, Children's Memorial Hospital, Chicago, and Associate Professor of Surgery, Northwestern University Medical School.

The incidence of meningomyelocele in the United States is about two per 1,000 live births, which makes it one of the most common congenital neurologic disorders. The inheritance is not Mendelian, but rather polygenetic in form, and the condition is often familial. There is certainly an ethnic influence, with an incidence greater than four per 1,000 live births in the Irish and Welsh, and less than one per 1,000 live births in Jews. If a couple has a child afflicted with meningomyelocele, the risk to a subsequent child rises to 5 percent, and if two children in a family are affected, the risk of a third child being affected is about 10 percent.[5]

In a consideration of treatment choices for the infant with meningomyelocele, one might first consider what will happen if the child is left untreated. Before this can be done, however, one must define the word "untreated." If by this term one means that the child is sedated and fed only on demand (the sedation apparently for the purpose of decreasing such demand) then the mortality rate is very high, ranging from 90 to 100 percent in the first year or two of life, the child usually succumbing to meningitis.[6] This method of nontreatment, we feel, represents passive euthanasia and is unacceptable. If by "untreated" one means providing only supportive care for the child in the form of proper nourishment and appropriate medications but withholding surgical therapy, then the mortality rate drops to 60–80 percent.[7] A striking feature of this statistic, however, is not so much the mortality rate, but the surprisingly high percentage of children who do survive. It follows, then, that if this form of nontreatment is advocated, one must be prepared to deal with the child who survives.

When in the 1960s the appeal for aggressive treatment of these children occurred in England,[8] it was hoped that this approach would increase the overall quality of survival. Unfortunately, this was not the case.[9] This then led some clinicians to attempt to establish guidelines that at birth they hoped would be predictive of the ultimate quality of survival and thereby allow a rational approach to treatment options.[10] The criteria that favored nontreatment consisted of (1) the presence of a meningomyelocele lesion with paralysis at the lumbar 2–3 level or above; (2) severe hydrocephalus at birth; (3) kyphosis of the spine; and (4) the presence of other congenital anomalies. The fallacy of trying to establish such criteria is rather easy to point out. First of all, the true motor level of a newborn infant with meningomyelocele is difficult enough to assess and, at birth, it is almost impossible to predict which of these children will eventually become ambulatory and competitive.[11] Furthermore, our data indicate that many of these children improve in motor function following early aggressive surgical treatment of the lesion. Second, as will also be pointed out later, the presence of hydrocephalus at birth is in itself not a significant factor in determining ultimate intellectual outcome. Third, modern surgical techniques have now made it possible to deal with the kyphotic spine frequently accompanying this anomaly.[12] Fourth, congenital anomalies affecting other organ systems in the child with meningomyelocele are rare.[13]

If one opts for aggressive surgical and medical treatment of these children, what kind of results can be expected? Again, a definition of terms is appropriate. We believe that the most important factor in "aggressive" surgical and medical treatment of these children involves a team approach to their multifaceted problems, utilizing the resources of neurosurgeons, orthopedic surgeons, urologists, neonatologists, pediatricians, psychologists, nurses, occupational therapists, physical therapists, social workers, dieticians, and, in particular, a meningomyelocele team coordinator. After initial evaluation by the neonatologist or pediatrician, the most urgent matter facing the team is neurosurgical closure of the meningomyelocele lesion to prevent cerebrospinal fluid leakage and possible meningitis. Our approach has been an early closure of the back wound (preferably within the first twenty-four hours). By closure, we do not mean merely covering the lesion with viable skin to prevent leakage of spinal fluid, but rather a true reconstruction of the neural tube itself, followed by wound closure in anatomical layers, including the arachnoid, dura, fascia, and skin.[14] Another neurosurgical problem common in meningomyelocele is the development of hydrocephalus. When it is evident that hydrocephalus is present and progressive, then we believe that extracranial cerebrospinal fluid diversionary procedures (shunts) should be inserted, and that these shunts should be aggressively revised when evidence of malfunction exists.

Early orthopedic evaluation and management of such commonly associated problems as clubbed feet and dislocated hips is equally important. Urologic evaluation of bladder function (and tests for urinary tract infection) are also important. Additionally, careful neonatologic follow-up for the myriad of medical problems that can affect any newborn, particularly one with a congenital anomaly, is necessary. Lastly, expert nursing care, along with frequent evaluations by psychologists, occupational therapists, physical therapists, dieticians, and social workers—all under the direction of a meningomyelocele team coordinator—can make such an "aggressive" approach fruitful, as we will attempt to demonstrate.

The following data, compiled from an intensive study of one hundred patients with meningomyelocele, are presented for illustration. All the patients were treated at the meningomyelocele clinic at Children's Memorial Hospital, Chicago, with two to six years' follow-up. These one hundred patients were consecutive and unselected; that is, all such patients with meningomyelocele admitted to the hospital during that time were aggressively treated, and none were selected out for supportive care only. (We will refer to these patients collectively as the sample group.)

Preoperatively, the level of the back lesion was thoracic in 24 percent of the patients, lumbar in 55 percent, and sacral in 21 percent. This percentage of sacral lesions is somewhat high and may possibly be due to a greater tendency to refer for treatment those children with sacral lesions and, consequently, less motor impairment. Eighty-six percent of the back wounds were closed within twenty-four hours of birth. We feel that this is important because, after that time, the skin becomes heavily colonized with bacteria,[15] increasing the incidence of both back-wound infections and subsequent shunt infections. A few back-wound infections did occur, but all were superficial and none led to significant wound dehiscence or meningitis. Postoperatively, the motor level was unchanged in 60 percent of the patients, improved in 37 percent, and worsened in 3 percent. These postoperative motor levels were maintained on subsequent examinations during the follow-up period. We would not, however, be so presumptuous as to claim that this rate of improvement was due to the surgical technique of reconstructing the neural tube. In fact, the 37 percent improvement rate may be due in large part to the resolution of spinal shock that is presumed to be present at birth in many of these children.

Seventy-five percent of the sample group went on to develop hydrocephalus. As mentioned, shunts were performed when the diagnosis was evident and the course progressive. Immediate shunt revision for obvious malfunction was also part of our aggressive surgical approach.

The surgical mortality was 2 percent: one infant died of necrotizing enterocolitis, and the other of profound hypoproteinemia. The overall mortality at five years' follow-up was 9 percent. It was also judged that another 11 percent of the sample group would not be competitive because of such limitations as profoundly poor intellectual development, tracheostomies, gastrostomies, and the like.

After considering the overall mortality and the percentage of children who were felt not likely to be competitive, we believe that we had good results in 80 percent of the children. Although no significance was found between the likelihood of developing hydrocephalus and the length of time that ensued before the back wound was closed, infections resulting from shunts performed as a treatment for hydrocephalus were three times greater if closure was accomplished more than twenty-four hours after birth. There was also significance between the development of hydrocephalus and the level of the meningomyelocele lesion, the incidence of hydrocephalus being greater the higher the level of the back lesion.

In addition to motor function, another important consideration in children born with meningomyelocele is intellectual outcome. The majority of studies in the past decade have shown a significant reduction in IQ when meningomyelocele is associated with hydrocephalus severe enough to require a shunting procedure.[16] In an earlier report from our institution by Drs. Soare and Raimondi,[17] the mean IQ of children with meningomyelocele alone was 102, while that of children with meningomyelocele associated with hydrocephalus was 87. Viewed another way, 87 percent of those with meningomyelocele alone had IQs greater than 80, while only 63 percent of those with meningomyelocele and hydrocephalus had IQs above 80. In 1976, however, it was reported that the presence of a central nervous system (CNS) infection in shunted hydrocephalic children with meningomyelocele dramatically lowered the IQ when compared with those children who either required no shunt or who required a shunt but remained infection free.[18] This, then, led us to reassess the data of Soare and Raimondi, many of whose patients were included in the sample group, to see whether or not the presence of CNS infection would be an additional factor in intellectual outcome.

Accordingly, patients of the sample group were placed into one of three subgroups: (1) not shunted, 39 patients; (2) shunted without CNS infection, 86 patients; and (3) shunted with CNS infection, 42 patients. No patient sustained a CNS infection who did not have a shunt. As mentioned, the mean IQ of those not requiring a shunt was 102 (range 50–140), the mean IQ for the general population being 100. The mean IQ of those who were shunted but remained infection free was 95 (range 20–140) – not significantly different from the nonshunted subgroup. Those children who were shunted and who then developed a CNS infection had a mean IQ of only 73 (range 10–140). This *is* significantly different from the other two subgroups. Viewed another way, of those who did not require a shunt, 87 percent had IQs greater than 80; of those shunted without infection, 80 percent had IQs greater than 80; and of those shunted with a CNS infection, only 31 percent had IQs over 80. Beyond the apparent deleterious effect of CNS infection on IQ, however, little further knowledge that was statistically significant could be determined from analysis of those so infected.

It is known that children with meningomyelocele suffer significant perceptual-motor deficiencies, and, in the report of Soare and Raimondi,[19] such deficiencies were found both in those with and those without accompanying hydrocephalus. In their study, the difference between chronologic age and perceptual-motor age for those with hydrocephalus was two years and for those without hydrocephalus 1.4 years – both statistically significant when compared wih their siblings. When CNS infection was taken into account, however, there was no difference between those without a shunt and those with an infection-free shunt as both subgroups showed a difference between chronologic age and perceptual-motor age of 1.4 years. Those children with CNS infection, however, showed a marked difference of 3.25 years between chronologic and perceptual-motor age.

Thus, it does not appear that the presence of hydrocephalus alone is a significant limiting factor in the ultimate intellectual development of children born with meningomyelocele. The result of infection upon the maturing central nervous system, however, is a significant factor, both in reducing the IQ and in enhancing the perceptual-motor deficits that exist in these children.

Meningomyelocele is a much more common birth defect than one might be led to believe. If left untreated, the result can be devastating for all concerned, particularly the child. Since we have found it virtually impossible to predict at birth which infants with meningomyelocele will become competitive, ambulatory, and intellectually able, we have not relied on arbitrary guidelines to determine which children should or should not be treated. On the contrary, we believe that all such children should be treated, and we feel that our data show this philosophy to be correct.

Notes

1. Shurtleff & Lamers, *Clinical Considerations in the Treatment of Myelodysplasia*, 20 U.C.L.A. FORUM MED. SCI. 103 (1978).

2. Nulsen and Spitz, *Treatment of Hydrocephalus by Direct Shunt from Ventricle to Jugular Vein*, 2 SURGICAL FORUM. 399 (1952).

3. Sharrard et al., *A Controlled Trial of Immediate and Delayed Closure of Spina Bifida Cystica*, 38 ARCHIVES DISEASE CHILDHOOD 18 (1963).

4. Brocklehurst, *The Pathogenesis of Spina Bifida: A Study of the Relationship Between Observation, Hypothesis and Surgical Incentive*, 13 DEVELOPMENTAL MED. CHILD NEUROLOGY SUPPLEMENT 147 (1971).

5. J. FREEMAN, PRACTICAL MANAGEMENT OF MENINGOMYELOCELE (1974). These statistics show that meningomyelocele is much more common than other well-known neurologic disorders such as polio, muscular dystrophy, and multiple sclerosis.

6. Hide, Williams, & Ellis, *The Outlook for the Child with a Myelomeningocele for Whom Early Surgery Was Considered Inadvisable*, 14 DEVELOPMENTAL MED. CHILD NEUROLOGY SUPPLEMENT 304 (1972); Lorber, *Results of Treatment of Myelomeningocele: An Analysis of 524 Unselected Cases with Special Reference to Possible Selection for Treatment*, 13 DEVELOPMENTAL MED. CHILD NEUROLOGY SUPPLEMENT 279 (1971).

7. Findlay, *An Appraisal of the Management of Spina Bifida Cystica*, 20 DEVELOPMENTAL MED. CHILD NEUROLOGY SUPPLEMENT 86 (1969); Knox, *Spina Bifida in Birmingham*, 13 DEVELOPMENTAL MED. CHILD NEUROLOGY SUPPLEMENT 14 (1967); Laurence, *The Survival of Untreated Spina Bifida Cystica*, 11 DEVELOPMENTAL MED. CHILD NEUROLOGY SUPPLEMENT 10 (1966); Shurtleff et al., *Myelodysplasia: Decision for Death or Disability*, 291 NEW ENGLAND J. MED. 1005 (1974).

8. Sharrard et al., *supra* note 3.

9. Lorber, *supra* note 6.

10. *Id.*

11. Ames & Schut, *Results of Treatment of 171 Consecutive Myelomeningoceles—1963 to 1968*, 50 PEDIATRICS 466 (1972); D. MATSON, NEUROSURGERY OF INFANCY AND CHILDHOOD (1969); Shurtleff et al., *supra* note 7.

12. Reigel, *Kyphectomy and Myelomeningocele Repair*, 13 MODERN TECHNIQUES IN SURGERY 1 (1979) (Neurosurgery).

13. Stein, Schut, & Ames, *Selection for Early Treatment in Myelomeningocele: A Retrospective Analysis of Various Selection Procedures,* 54 PEDIATRICS 553 (1974).

14. McLone, *Technique for Closure of Myelomeningocele,* 6 CHILD'S BRAIN 65 (1980).

15. Raine & Young, *Bacterial Colonisation and Infection in Lesions of the Central Nervous System,* 35 DEVELOPMENTAL MED. CHILD NEUROLOGY SUPPLEMENT 111 (1975).

16. Spain, *Verbal and Performance Ability in Pre-school Children with Spina Bifida,* 16 DEVELOPMENTAL MED. CHILD NEUROLOGY SUPPLEMENT 773 (1974); Tew & Laurence, *The Effects of Hydrocephalus on Intelligence, Visual Perception and School Attainment,* 17 DEVELOPMENTAL MED. CHILD NEUROLOGY SUPPLEMENT 129 (1975).

17. Soare & Raimondi, *Intellectual and Perceptual-motor Characteristics of Treated Myelomeningocele Children,* 131 AM. J. DISEASES CHILDREN 199 (1977).

18. Hunt & Holmes, *Factors Relating to Intelligence In Treated Cases of Spina Bifida Cystica,* 130 AM. J. DIS. CHILD. 823 (1976).

19. Soare & Raimondi, *supra* note 17.

7
A General Theory
of Retardation

Jérôme LeJeune

It seems that a dilemma exists in the civilized world today: to kill or to heal. The answer is, of course, to heal. This chapter argues, in technical terms, that healing of the seriously retarded is beginning to be possible.

Because it can be caused by so many different diseases, mental retardation is, strictly speaking, not a disease but a symptom. Out of the formidable array of congenital afflictions that can produce mental retardation, we can make some order and glean some understanding if we first ask ourselves about the substratum of the intelligence, that is, the "wiring" of our brain.

When Pascal discovered that arithmetic calculation could be simulated by the play of gears and rods correctly arranged in a little machine, he demonstrated at the same time that logic can be inserted in matter if matter is properly shaped. Nowadays, computers are much more complicated, but no matter what kind of procedure they use to manage matter and energy, they must fulfill three very simple requirements. These three are the same for any machine, whether it is a pocket calculator or a huge and complex computer used to put a man into space. The three requirements are: (1) there is a preestablished, logically constructed network; (2) inside the machine there are clear, diffusion-free transmissions; and (3) each element of the machine answers clearly and without inertia or hesitation.

I do not claim that what you have in your braincase is a kind of computer, but the way we have built the machine shows us that the same breakdown that can impair the functioning of a computer can occur in human pathology to damage the efficiency of the brain. It is with that model that we can attempt to understand what mental retardation is.

Our brain greatly outclasses any actual or foreseeable machine. We have some eleven billion neurons inside our brain interconnected by some

Jérôme LeJeune, M.D., is Chairman, Department of Fundamental Genetics, University of Paris. He is a recipient of the William Allan Memorial Award, American Society of Human Genetics. He is credited with the discovery of the cause of Down's syndrome and has done extensive research on possible treatments for Down's syndrome.

eleven trillion contacts called synapses—components in number and complexity of a far greater magnitude than the biggest computer system ever built. If we look at the links in the network of wiring inside our brain, the number is astronomical. If you disentangled all the small neural fibers which intercommunicate between the cells and laid them end to end, they would go from Chicago to Mexico City without difficulty. But if you took the tiny fibers which are inside the cellular process and which constitute the very wiring of the brain and laid *them* end to end, they would go to the moon and possibly back. That gives you an idea of the complexity of this marvelous machine that is working inside our head.

A repairman opening a big computer which does not work is in exactly the same situation as a neurologist examining a mentally retarded child. For example, our repairman could observe easily that a rack of electronics has been burned, and that the machine does not work because part of it has been destroyed. In like manner a neurologist might determine that one of several diseases has caused a progressive destruction of part of the brain—either by an infection, a trauma, or by the hydraulic pressure of hydrocephalia (which laminates the brain)—which has reduced enormously the efficiency of the substratum of the mentally retarded child's intelligence.

Sometimes it is a part of the machine itself which has not been built during embryonic development. Neural tube defects are of utmost importance in understanding this type of mistake. At the beginning of life—around ten days—the first line appears on the embryo showing where the neural tube will grow. Once the tube begins to grow the closing continues in both directions, exactly like a zip system going both up and down. If it does not close at one end, you get spina bifida or meningomyelocele; if it does not close at the other end, you get an aplasia of the cerebellum and eventually anencephaly, that is, an absence of the brain. Anencephalic children cannot survive because they do not have the ability to regulate themselves since their system has not been built.

Interestingly, climate apparently has a major effect on the incidence of neural tube defects. The disease is rather rare in the south, but it increases as you go north. This is very true in Great Britain, for example. There are many more cases in Scotland than around London. Neural tube defects are very rare in Sicily, but the frequency increases when you come to France, and there is a gradient within that country, increasing as you go north.

The climate-related nature of the disorder is the first characteristic that does not fit what is normal of genetic disease. The second is that there is a very curious familial and sociological distribution of the disease. Low-income parents in a given town have a greater risk of having afflicted children than do the rich. Also, when a mother has an afflicted child, the risk of the next child being afflicted is increased. For example, in Ireland the risk is 0.2 percent for the population as a whole, but if a mother already has a child afflicted with neural tube defect, the risk for the next child is around 5 percent—twenty-five times greater. But what is again very surprising is that if the mother is rich, the risk is lower than 5 percent; if the mother is poor, the risk is greater than 5 percent.

A discovery in England in 1971 further complicates the picture. That year there was harvested a blighted crop of potatoes. Normally, blighted potatoes are given to the pigs, but that year they were sold on the market, and a very curious statistical trend emerged: among the mothers who had children afflicted with neural tube defect that year, many had consumed blighted potatoes, but far fewer mothers of healthy children had eaten the potatoes.[1] It was then believed that it was a poisonous substance causing the defect. Unfortunately it was not; you cannot produce neural tube defect with blighted potatoes. The mystery was growing deeper when it was discovered that when a neural tube does not close, alpha-fetoprotein leaks into the amniotic fluid; from the amniotic fluid it can penetrate the blood of the mother. With a special alpha-fetoprotein kit one can determine the level of that substance in the mother's blood to confirm the suspicion of neural tube defect by examining the amniotic fluid.

In 1976 an enormous and very costly program was begun in England (a program I understand is being considered in the United States also) to screen every pregnant woman for alpha-fetoprotein. They are now going to be able to screen half of the would-be mothers in England in order to detect if the child has a problem, then kill the baby if he or she is afflicted. But the story does not stop here; it is just beginning.

In 1980 R. W. Smithells from Leeds, England, published the first data about prevention of neural tube defect. From his own research and in light of the discovery in 1968 of Hibbard and Hibbard (who had found that mothers of children affected by neural tube defect had a low level of folic acid in their blood),[2] Smithells concluded that he should treat future mothers with a special diet containing folic acid and a few other vitamins—such treatment to begin, where possible, before conception. Smithells selected two samples of mothers who had previously delivered an afflicted child. Of the two samples, one received the vitamin therapy and the other did not. The outcome was that of the 178 children born from treated mothers, only one was afflicted with neural tube defect. Remember that the risk was 5 percent and that eight or nine afflicted babies were expected. On the other hand, of 260 pregnancies of the untreated mothers there were 13 neural tube defect children—exactly the 5 percent expected.[3]

Smithells's study apparently explains the previously cited epidemiology of the disease. Folic acid is found on the leaf of fresh vegetables. The further north you go, the fewer fresh vegetables are available in winter, and the resulting higher prices of fresh vegetables even further restricts their purchase by the poor. Additionally, the boiling of fresh vegetables, a common cooking method in England, like the canning process, destroys folic acid. Therefore, Smithells's study strongly indicates that the most purely sporadic cases of congenital neural tube defects are due to a preventable abnormality in the metabolism of the folic acid system.[4]

Curiously, even abortionists could have added a stone to this castle. Unwillingly, J. B. Thiersch stumbled over it around twenty-five years ago. Thiersch wanted to induce so-called therapeutic abortions. (By the way, there are no therapeutic abortions because abortion kills the baby virtually 100 percent of the time, and a therapy which kills the patient 100 percent of the time is not a therapy.) He tried to kill the babies by giving the mother aminopterine, a very powerful drug which impedes the normal action of folic acid (aminopterine is classified as an anti-folic acid). He succeeded, but a few of the babies managed one way or another to survive and some of the surviving ones had some type of neural tube defect.[5] Unfortunately, had these results been properly analyzed, research on prevention could have started a quarter of a century earlier. But fighting *against* life is a type of medicine that blindfolds: the relevance of facts, even correctly observed, remains unrecognized.

The second requirement is to prevent short circuitry inside the network. To prevent it, nature folds around the small fibers of all the nerves inside our brain a kind of insulating substance that we call myelin. There is a vast array of diseases in which the building up or breaking down of the molecular components of the myelin is deficient, so that intermediate products which should be transformed into the myelin accumulate in the cell and kill it, producing severe neurological damage. For example, Tay-Sachs disease, which is exceedingly rare (about 20 cases a year in the United States), can produce very severe degeneration of the brain just because the myelin is not perfectly used. We know of many other afflictions, each of them very rare, which are due to this difficulty of handling the insulators inside our brain. There are, for example, Niemann-Pick disease, Gaucher's disease, Krabbe's disease, and metachromatic leukodystrophy.

We know that destruction of the network or trouble with the insulating system cannot explain the vast majority of cases of mental retardation because in most cases there is a brain which is more or less normal, that is, it may have some imperfection but it is basically normal. What happens is that the brain apparently does not run at top speed. It runs, but not at the full speed we expect of it.

The brain runs just the way a computer does; that is, each of the connections is in fact the equivalent of a gate, and as we say in France, *"il faut qu'une porte soit ouverte ou fermée"*—a door must be either open or closed. That is the basis of pure logic: the interdiction against being something and not being it at the same time. When you make a succession of steps in your thoughts, you are obliged to go from one, which is like this, to another, which is like that and not like any other; logic requires saying yes or no at every step of your reasoning. The binary logic used by computers does the same thing. What is important is the speed with which those little gates can open and close. Very likely, when you just say a word, you travel a few kilometers along the wiring of your brain without knowing it.

The speed with which the transmission is achieved through all those gates is of the utmost importance; we can understand that just by looking at babies. For example, a baby afflicted with Down's syndrome is a little weak, a little hypotonic. His look is also a little weak, a little floppy. It is not very sharp; it has fatigue in it. But what is much more evident is that he cannot close his mouth. When he is very young his mouth is open and his tongue is out most of the time. This is because he cannot go fast enough along his own nervous network. He just does what any traffic agency would do in a big town. When there is a traffic jam—that is, when the speed with which the cars are going through the streets is slow because there are too many cars—there is only one solution: access to some highways must be closed temporarily so that people already on them can go on. When a person is using all the power of his intellect to admire a painting or statue or to listen to wonderful music, he is agape. Because he is using all his power, he has no power left to think about giving an order to the muscle of his mandible to close his mouth. The power to use his brain is limited and he must close down some highways so that he can have enough fluid circulation to concentrate fully on the piece of art.

Every one of us knows that we cannot think at a great speed. For example, when we want to be sure of what we are thinking about, we must go step by step. If we try to go too fast, we cannot follow ourselves. We can accept the fact that we cannot go very fast, but if we try to think of something very slowly and we slow down the path of our minds, suddenly another idea goes through our minds and we lose our train of thought. That is proof that for using our brain we cannot use first gear, second gear, or third gear at will, but rather we must use that speed at which the brain functions best.

There are, of course, significant differences in the particular structures of computers and our brains. One difference is that, unlike the gates in electric circuitry, it is not an electric current that goes from one cell to the next. At the end of one cell a molecule called the chemical mediator is ejected. When this molecule (acetylocholine, noradrenalin, serotonin, et cetera) comes to the surface of the next cell, it changes the property of that cell, which suddenly becomes able to engulf some special ions; that is, to count them particle by particle.[6] So we have in our brain a kind of geiger counter, but one which is much more efficient than any geiger counter invented so far.

To perform properly, each cell has to give the right molecule to the next cell. This system closely resembles a security key that will go only in one lock and will not be accepted by any other. In our brain each cell is able to emit a special molecule which will be understood only by a given type of cell and not by others. This specificity of molecules makes it possible to identify functional systems within the complicated tangle of networks. These functional systems probably correspond to the major cerebral functions (motor system, pain transmission system, mood regulation, et cetera) and each uses its own personal molecular language. It is this specificity that enables us to understand the pharmacological activity of certain drugs affecting almost exclusively one system or another.

It is clear that the molecular machinery must be extremely precise in order to manufacture the right amount of the mediator molecule—at the right time and in the right place—and to then ensure its disposal or recovery. It is therefore possible that many mental deficiencies (in which there is neither gross anatomical decay nor lesions on the insulating sheaths of the nerves) are the result of problems in supplying the necessary mediators to the proper location.

The Monocarbon Hypothesis. Monocarbons are tiny molecules containing only one atom of carbon; their purpose is to methylate particular molecules (phospholipids). This transmethylation process is as complex as it is crucial. In some development processes every molecule must be methylated three times. For example, in the manufacture of myelin, three monocarbons are used to make one molecule of insulating substance. Another example is the manufacture of the mediator molecules. To make any security key to open the locks we again have to methylate three times. This explains why in every disease in which we find mental retardation due to a blockage that we know chemically, the monocarbon system is not running at a proper speed.

It is clear that monocarbons are the smallest building blocks in the cerebral edifice. They are also the most frequently used and are found in very diverse locations. From this we can arrive at the general hypothesis (the "monocarbon hypothesis") that problems in providing raw material (forerunners of monocarbons), in transporting monocarbons (folic acid cycle), or in the utilization of monocarbons (methyl transfer or transmethylation), may be key factors in mental retardation.[7]

A double argument reinforces this point of view. First, the brain has a kind of folic acid pump—such that the cerebral concentration is always greater (as much as four times greater) than that in the rest of the human body. For example, even in the case of folic acid deficiency the level in the liver falls long before the cerebral reserve is tapped. Second, all diseases which block transformations of folic acid or which block the transport of monocarbons to transmethylation bring on all the formidable neurological syndromes.[8]

This general hypothesis (proposed in 1979 but apparently not accepted because nobody noticed it) seems to fit with the data that have been accumulated since that time. The effect of folic acid on neural tube defects is explained by the fact that during the building of the brain we need a fantastic number of monocarbons in order to build both the insulating system and the special protein inside. If there is suddenly a shortage of folic acid, which is the monocarbon transporter, the brain is shorted the necessary number of such carriers. Evidently, when there are no carriers at all, the brain is not developed—as in the case of full anencephaly.

Disorders caused by chromosomal aberrations are difficult to fit into the monocarbon hypothesis of mental retardation. As a full discussion of chromosomal pathology would be far too voluminous, only one, representative, such disorder will be examined here—trisomy 21, or Down's syndrome.

Occasionally a woman experiences what is known as a translocation; that is, one of her chromosome 21's has been cut in two pieces and one of the pieces has been translocated to another chromosome. Although she is perfectly normal (the fact that her chromosome 21 is split does not affect her), a child she bears might be afflicted with trisomy 21 because he received not only two normal chromosomes but also the untranslocated piece from the mother. An excess quantity of genetic material produces the disease.

In other cases the mother has one normal 21 but the other 21 has received a part of chromosome 15, and part of chromosome 21 has translocated to chromosome 15. Again, the mother is perfectly normal although she does not have the correct distribution of genes. One of her children would receive a normal 21 and a 15 with an extra piece, so the child is now trisomic, but not for the whole chromosome 21, only for the end part of it. On the other hand, another child of this mother would receive normal 21's and normal 15's, but would also receive the extra piece, from the top of chromosome 21, not the end of it.

In the case of a girl who carries the same translocation as the mother, she is perfectly normal. Perhaps her sister would receive the extra piece of chromosome 21, but the one which is close to the top. She has no Down's syndrome whatsoever, but she has a mild mental deficiency—a very curious one with a little touch of autism.

Families where parent(s) and children both have abnormal 21's are extremely rare, but among the 3,000 cases we are following, even rare events are expected. We can summarize it as follows: When children have an excess of the top part, they do not show Down's syndrome. They are not normal, but they do not have Down's syndrome. When they have too much of the *end* piece they too show no Down's syndrome, but when they are carrying that piece in the middle (designated 9221) they show the full syndrome. The disease is thus related to a tiny part of the chromosome.

We can go deeper than that. We know four functions, four chemical reactions, that are going too fast because of this extra chromosome: Superoxide dismutase (SOD 1), located in zone Q221,[9] is 1.5 times as active in persons afflicted with Down's syndrome[10] as it is in persons not afflicted with the disorder. The same is true for glycinamide ribonucleotide synthetase[11] and possibly for 5-aminolevulinate dyhydratase. A fourth gene is known to be on chromosome 21: the one which controls the manufacture of a protein sensitive to interferon.[12]

Why should these speeded-up chemical reactions affect intelligence? For example, suppose that the genes are the musicians of an orchestra. Suppose also that when there are, as is normal, two musicians for one position (that is, we have two chromosomes—one from the father and one from the mother), they go at a given speed. But if there are three musicians (like in trisomy 21, where there is one chromosome too many), there is one too many, and they go a little too fast. They don't play louder; they play faster. The result is very interesting because when we compare children who have an excess of a chromosome to children who are missing part of the same chromosome, we find that their morphologies are the opposite of one another. For example, trisomy 21 children have small ears and a flat nose; children who are lacking part of chromosome 21 have a prominent nose and big ears. So, an excess of chromosome gives the opposite effect as that produced by a deficiency of the chromosome. But where intelligence is concerned it does not matter whether there is not enough of a chromosome or too much of it. The result is the same: mental retardation.

Life is a kind of music and genes are a kind of musician. When we look at a morphological trait we are looking at something directed by one gene. Suppose that we have the whole orchestra playing the symphony of life. Suppose further that one musician goes faster than the tempo of the orchestra. If this musician executes a solo, the solo will be changed. Instead of *andante* it will be *presto*. But that will not destroy the symphony; it will just change one of the traits of the symphony. On the other hand, if the musician is not playing at the same speed as the rest of the orchestra at a time when all the instruments are playing together, the result—whether the off-tempo musician is playing too slowly or too quickly—is cacophony. It is what produces the equivalent of mental retardation because the human mind is the most complicated thing that living systems have been able to sustain. There is no other thing in the world as complicated as our brain; for its proper running we obviously need the full interplay of all the elements of our genetic endowment. If something is going too fast or too slow, the main property of the system, which is the efficiency of the intelligence, is affected.

An analysis of comparative pathology, that is, illnesses in which certain major symptoms resemble some of those of trisomy 21 (hypothyroidism, iminodipeptiduria, Alzheimer's disease, Lesh Nyhan disease, et cetera), or in which the symptoms are the opposite of trisomy 21 (homocystinuria, for example), permits saying that the probability of monocarbon deficiency in trisomy 21 is very great.[13]

Another chromosomal disease, which is *a priori* quite different from trisomy 21, seems to offer an excellent opportunity for research on the role of monocarbons. In this disorder, called Xqfra syndrome, there is a fragile zone of the distal part of the long arm of the X chromosome, hence the name Xqfra. A culture medium low in folic acid very often causes a gap on the X chromosome. But in a culture medium enriched with folic acid or formyltetrahydrofolate, the fragile zone remains unaffected.[14] This discovery was recently confirmed and enlarged upon: adding monocarbon precursors (such as serine and hydroxyproline) to a culture medium low in folic acid can also prevent the appearance of the gap.[15]

Suppose we are dealing with a school; the school is our brain. There are buses to take the children from their homes to school. The children are the monocarbons, the tiny molecules. But the children have to stay in the houses, which are the precursors of monocarbons. It is the monocarbons which can cure the disease. The bus is the folic acid; it transfers the children to the school. If the buses are not in service, the children cannot go from their homes to school. The school is empty. The folic acid has not brought the monocarbons to the brain.

There is another possible disease in which the doors of the homes are closed. The buses are running but the children cannot go out of their houses because the doors are closed. In that case the school is again empty. It is not the same disease because there are so many different doors to so many different houses. If you number each of the doors you will find an enormous number of diseases, each apparently entirely different, which prevent the children from going to school. That is what really happens in mental retardation.

Although it seems clear that monocarbon metabolism plays a significant role in mental retardation, it is too early to say that the results obtained *in vitro* can be applied *in vivo,* that is, that they will lead to a systematic, effective treatment. However, neuropsychological correlations between the utilization of folic acid derivatives and the functioning of the brain have already been found.[16]

But what can we do for the children? The answer to that question cannot be determined until a very long clinical trial has been conducted. All that can be stated safely is that in the few cases in which we have treated trisomy 21 children we have achieved positive results. We have treated these children in a double blind test, giving them serine. Serine is an ordinary amino acid, totally nontoxic, but one that can produce monocarbons. Children whose diets are enriched with serine do slightly better during the next six months than children who receive a placebo.[17] This does not mean that the treatment has been found. It means simply that we can transfer a general hypothesis to clinical investigation to see what the effect is. This is very painstaking and very time consuming. For example, to test three substances normally found in food in very small quantities, 120 children must be tested for one year in order to accurately measure just how much intellectual gain there might be. Still, we hope that this type of research will lead to a cure.

* * *

We do not know if the cure will come tomorrow, the next day, next year, in ten years, or in fifty years. And we can do nothing to make time go faster. But we can nevertheless do something.

A man named Liautey wanted to improve the economy in his country and was wondering what he could do. After consultation he decided that the best thing was to plant more date trees because his people so much loved dates there were never enough to meet the demand. But his counselors told him to remember that it takes twenty years before a date tree begins to bear fruit. Liautey said, "Are you really sure it takes twenty years?" When they answered affirmatively, he replied, "Then, we begin today."

Notes

1. Renwick, *Hypothesis: Anenencephaly and Spina Bifida Are Usually Preventable by Avoidance of a Specific but Unidentified Substance Present in Certain Potato Tubers,* 26 BRITISH J. PREVENTIVE & SOC. MED. 67 (1972).

2. Hibbard & Hibbard, *Folate Metabolism and Reproduction,* 24 BRITISH MED. BULL. 10–12 (1968).

3. Smithells, Sheppard, Schoran, et al., *Possible Prevention of Neural-Tube Defects by Periconceptional Vitamin Supplementation,* LANCET, Feb. 16, 1980, at 339–40.

4. The Smithells et al. study has been confirmed in part by Laurence, James, Miller, Tennant, & Campbell in their study, *Double-blind Randomised Controlled Trial of Folate Treatment before Conception to Prevent Recurrence of Neural-Tube Defects,* 282 BRITISH MED. J. 1509–11 (1981).

5. Thiersch, *Therapeutic Abortions with a Folic Acid Atagonist, 4-Aminopteroylglutamic Acid (4-Amino G.P.A.) Administered by the Oral Route,* 63 AM. J. OBSTETRICS & GYNECOLOGY 1298–1304 (1952 vol. II); Thiersch, *The Control of Reproduction in Rats with the Aid of Antimetabolites; Early Experiences with Antimetabolites as Abortifaciond Agents in Man,* Acta Endocrinologica 37 (1956 Supp. 28).

6. LeJeune, *Is the Sodium Ionic Channel a Cyclic Hexapeptide?,* 22 ANNALES DE GÉNÉTIQUE 108 (1979).

7. LeJeune, *Biochemical Investigations and Trisomy 21,* 22 ANNALES DE GÉNÉTIQUE 67–75 (1975) [hereinafter cited as LeJeune, *Biochemical Investigations*].

8. Rowe, *Inherited Disorders of Folate Metabolism,* in THE METABOLIC BASIS OF INHERITED DISEASE 430 (4th ed. J. Stanbury, J. Wyngaarden, & D. Frederickson eds. 1978).

9. Sinet, LeJeune, & Jerome, *Trisomy 21 (Down's syndrome): Glutathrone Peroxidase, Hexose Monophosphate Shunt and I.Q.,* 24 LIFE SCI. 29 (1979) [hereinafter cited as Sinet et al., *Trisomy 21*].

10. Sinet, Allard, LeJeune, & Jerome, *Augmentation d'Activité de la Superoxyde Dismutase E'rthrocytaire dans la Trisomie pour le Chromosome 21,* 278 COMPTES RENDUS DE L'ACADEMIE DES SCIENCES 3267 (1974).

11. Sinet et al., *Trisomy 21, supra* note 9, at 29–34. See also Moore, Jines, Kao, & Dates, *Synteny between Glycinamide Ribonucleotide Synthetase and Superoxide Dismutase (Soluable),* 29 AM. J. HUMAN GENETICS 389, 391 (1977); Bartley & Epstein, *Gene Dosage Effect for Glycinamide Ribonucleotide Synthetase in Human Fibroblasts Trisomic for Chromosome 21,* 93 BIOCHEMISTRY & BIOPHYSICS RESEARCH COMMITTEE 1286 (1980).

12. J. Grouchy & C. Turlean, CLINICAL ATLAS OF HUMAN CHROMOSOMES 187–209 (1977).

13. LeJeune, *Biochemical Investigations, supra* note 7, at 76-75.

14. Sutherland, *Heritable Fragile Sites on Human Chromosomes,* 31 AM. J. HUMAN GENETICS 125 (1979).

15. LeJeune, *Fragile Site X_q27 and Metabolism of Monocarbons,* 22 ANNALES DE GÉNÉTIQUE 1075 (1980). Recent research indicates that folic acid administration to patients themselves not only protects the fragile zone of their X chromosome, but also seems to improve their mental status. LeJeune, *Fragile Site X_q27 and Metabolism of Monocarbons: Significant Decrease of the Frequency of Chromosomal Gaps by Treatment In Vitro and In Vivo,* 292 COMPTES RENDUS DE L'ACADEMIE DES SCIENCES 491 (1981).

16. Botez, Botez, Leveille, Bielmann, & Cadotte, *Neuropsychological Correlates of Folic Acid Deficiency: Facts and Hypotheses,* in FOLIC ACID IN NEUROLOGY, PSYCHIATRY, AND INTERNAL MEDICINE 435 (1979).

17. LeJeune, unpublished data.

8

Ethical and Surgical Considerations in the Care of the Newborn with Congenital Abnormalities

C. Everett Koop

The medical profession has traditionally made its treatment of patients a reflection of society's concern for those who are ill or helpless. Often the profession has acted as advocate for those who had no one else to stand up for them. In the Hippocratic tradition and in line with the Judeo-Christian ethic, the medical profession responded with love and compassion toward the helpless child.

There was a day when medicine was not only a profession but was considered to be an art. There were even those who considered it to be a calling such as the ministry. A man who practiced medicine was called to a compassionate ethic that led him to the service of his fellowman. He worked in diagnosis and treatment in the realm of trust between the patient and himself. When he dealt with a child or an incompetent adult, he dealt in the realm of trust between the patient's family and himself.

One of the distortions in society which will not benefit any family is a change in semantics and hence philosophy in the practice of medicine. The semantic change that has crept into medicine is one in which the patient is called the "consumer"—as though he were eating cereal. The physician is called a "provider"—as though he were delivering gasoline. We refer to the "health care delivery system" as though it were some monolithic structure from which the consumer had the right to expect only success. Delivery systems and consumers imply contracts. Contracts imply restrictions, and the restrictions that are implied are not just on the physician; they end up as restrictions on the type of health care actually delivered—the very thing the system is seeking to avoid by the semantic change. (I will return to semantics several times during the course of this chapter.)

C. Everett Koop graduated from Dartmouth College, received his M.D. from Cornell Medical School and his Sc.D. (medicine) from the University of Pennsylvania. He is currently the Surgeon General of the United States. Formerly he was Surgeon-in-Chief, Children's Hospital of Philadelphia; Professor of Pediatrics and Pediatric Surgery, University of Pennsylvania School of Medicine; and Editor-in-Chief, *Journal of Pediatric Surgery.*

One of the complications of this change toward consumerism is the expectancy of perfection. There was a day when the patient (not the consumer) had confidence that his physician was practicing in the realm of trust, and knew he was going to get the best his physician could possibly accomplish. Now, after the provider has outlined for the consumer what his expectancy is from the ensuing relationship, if the result is either less than perfection or less than the provider's estimate of his approach to perfection, then the consumer feels it is his right to be compensated for the discrepancy. The only way he can be compensated is by a financial reward following a malpractice litigation. Human bodies are not like carburetors; the same thing does not affect all patients in the same way. There is an inherent failure rate in all that the physician seeks to accomplish.

Infanticide is the killing of a born infant by direct means or by withholding something necessary for its survival. This practice in the United States is extraordinarily important to those who are interested in the sanctity of human life because infanticide might never have come about had it not been for abortion on demand. When I read, in the months following the January 22, 1973 decision of the Supreme Court in *Roe v. Wade,* various references to Justice Blackmun's majority opinion in that case, my blood ran cold. You will remember that he considered the Hippocratic Oath which forbids abortion to be irrelevant. He spurned whatever morality he might have gleaned from the Judeo-Christian heritage of this country and turned instead to the pagan religions of Rome, of Greece, and of Persia. Although those countries practiced abortion, it was infanticide and euthanasia which were more important inhumanities in their cultures.

The second important thing to remember about infanticide is that it is euthanasia in an age group. There are many semantic differences in the English language on both sides of the Atlantic and infanticide is one of them. Infanticide in Great Britain usually means the killing of a born infant by the infant's mother. Infanticide in this country is the killing of a born infant by medical personnel in a hospital either by a direct act or much more commonly by the withholding of something necessary for the survival of that infant. Its hidden importance in reference to our concerns in the future is that I am certain the day will come when the euthanasia forces will say, "Why are you concerned about euthanasia? We have had euthanasia of infants for a long time and there has been no outcry."

The third important thing concerning infanticide is that it is being practiced by a segment of the medical profession from whom we have traditionally expected more—pediatricians and pediatric surgeons—and it is being ignored by a segment of our society from whom the victim has a right to expect more—namely, the law.

The medical profession has slipped its anchor and drifted away from the commitment which put the patient first in the recognition of the fact that he needed the help a physician could provide. This principle was rather universally understood in medicine not too long ago when morality was based on certain absolutes that the individual perceived as right or wrong. I am distressed that in an era of moral relativism, the life of a handicapped child can be forfeited to alleviate suffering in the family. If the practice of infanticide is a perversion of the former morality in medicine, that is bad enough. But if the situation is compounded by the fact that the law has turned its back as though infanticide did not exist, then we are indeed in trouble, for who knows the direction the extension of this philosophy will take next?

For almost thirty-five years now I have devoted the major part of my professional life to the management of children born with a congenital defect. I was, however, a surgeon of the skin and its contents in my early years. Therefore, my experience with congenital defects is broader than just the field that ordinarily is now called general pediatric surgery. Although in my more recent years my interests have been confined to those congenital anomalies incompatible with life but nevertheless amenable to surgical correction, there was a day when I was concerned with the management of cleft lips and palates, orthopedic defects, spina bifida and its complications, congenital heart disease, and major urologic defects.

I know what can be accomplished in the habilitation of a child born less than perfect. I know what can be done with that child's family. I know that these children become loved and loving, that they are creative, and that their entrance into a family is frequently looked back upon in subsequent years as an extraordinarily positive experience. Those who never have had the privilege of working with handicapped children who are being habilitated into our society after the correction of a congenital defect frequently tell me that such a child should be allowed to die or even encouraged to die because its life could obviously be nothing but unhappy and miserable. Yet it has been my constant experience that disability and unhappiness do not go hand in hand. The most unhappy children I have known have been completely normal. On the other hand, there is remarkable joy and happiness in the lives of most handicapped children; yet some have borne burdens that I would have indeed found very difficult to endure.

The first medical effort I know of in this country to educate the profession in the management of a defective newborn where death was one of the options in treatment is the film *Who Shall Survive?* produced by the Joseph P. Kennedy Foundation.[1] It depicts the manner in which a child with both Down's syndrome and duodenal atresia was given nothing by mouth until it expired from dehydration and starvation fifteen days later. Whatever was the intent of those who produced and financed this film, when it is seen during orientation week by new medical students across the country it is interpreted as an acceptable example of the management of a difficult problem in neonatology.

The first medical article along these lines to attract wide attention is entitled "Dilemmas of the Newborn Intensive Care Nursery," by Drs. Raymond S. Duff and A. G. M. Campbell of Yale University School of Medicine.[2] They acknowledge that over a two-year period about 14 percent of the deaths in their special care unit were those they permitted to happen because it was their considered judgment after discussion with the family that these children's lives were not worth living. It is impossible for the physician not to influence the family by innuendo alone; how much more if he counsels: "If this were my own child. . . ." The written word can never truly compete with the spoken word in matters such as this. I have to acknowledge that when I read the Duff and Campbell report, my emotions were a combination of fury and frustration. Yet, when I talk with Dr. Duff, I recognize that we have different concerns, and probably different understandings, of the ethics of the situation. My focus is on the life of the child; his is on the well-being of the family. My ethics might be said to be based on moral rules concerning absolutes of right and wrong, whereas I would suspect that his ethical principles are based more on a balance between the advantages to the patient and the disadvantages to the family.

My concerns about death as an option in the management of a handicapped newborn are centered not only on withholding treatment from the patient, but also on the implications of this form of management when extended to other children and to adults. This is because I believe in the "thin edge of the wedge" theory and in the dangers of the "slippery slope," whereas Dr. Duff does not see the slippery slope in the same light.

Drs. Duff and Campbell state in their article: "Survivors of these neonatal intensive care units may be healthy and their parents grateful, but in some instances continue to suffer from such conditions as chronic pulmonary disease, short bowel syndrome or various manifestations of brain damage. Others are severely handicapped by a myriad of congenital malformations that in previous times have resulted in death."[3] Because a newborn child has the possibility of having dyspnea, oxygen dependence, incontinence, paralysis, a contracture, or a sexual handicap does not necessarily entitle the physician to decide that the child's life is not worth living. If we decide that this is a reason for terminating a child's life, how long will it be before the same thinking is extended to adults who already have these same signs and symptoms and might be considered candidates for some type of euthanasia program?

Drs. Duff and Campbell also state: "Often too, the parents' or siblings' rights to relief from the seemingly pointless, crushing burdens were important considerations."[4] It seems to me that this is solving a social problem by inattention to a newborn handicapped child resulting in his death. I do not think this is the proper use of medical expertise. As stated previously, society is the loser when the patient becomes the impersonal consumer and the profession is delivering a service.

When a double standard exists for the management of the newborn with a handicap, one can expect a double standard to follow for the care of the nonhandicapped newborns and for older patients as well. In response to the Duff and Campbell article, there appeared among letters to the editor in the same journal one by Drs. Joan L. Venes and Peter R. Huttenlocher of the Yale University School of Medicine.[5] They described themselves as some of the "specialists based in the medical center" referred to by Duff and Campbell. The letter concludes:

> As consultants to the newborn special care unit, we wish to dissociate ourselves from the opinions expressed by the authors. The "growing tendency to seek early death as a management option" that the authors referred to has been repeatedly called to the attention of those involved and has caused us deep concern. It is troubling to us to hear young pediatric interns ask first, "should we treat?" rather than "how do we treat?" We are fearful that this feeling of nihilism may not remain restricted to the newborn special care unit. To suggest that the financial and psychological stresses imposed upon a family with the birth of a handicapped child constitutes sufficient justification for such a therapy of nihilism is untenable and allows us to escape what perhaps after all are the real issues—i.e., the obligation of an affluent society to provide financial support and the opportunity for a gainful life to its less fortunate citizens.[6]

Even in my own institution where the ethical teaching has been quite different from that emanating from Yale, new house officers ask, on occasion, "Should we treat?" before they ask, "How should we treat?"

Publication of the Duff and Campbell article has accomplished two things: it has evoked response in rebuttal such as has already been quoted, and it has made the subject of what is called "the decision-making process" or "selection" possible to be further talked about and written about. For example, one headline in *Pediatric News* declares: "M.D.—Parent Decision Needed to Kill Infant."[7] This headline is in association with the Sonoma Conference on Ethical Issues held in 1975. A panel of twenty was almost unanimous in answering affirmatively to the following two questions: (1) Would it ever be right not to resuscitate an infant at birth?; and (2) Would it ever be right to withdraw life support from a clearly diagnosed poor prognosis infant? *Pediatric News,* in reporting on the conference, stated that the state of medical ethics in this area is not yet settled. Ethics are relative and change: morals are absolute and do not.

Dr. R. T. F. Schmidt of Cincinnati, at that time president-elect of the American College of Obstetricians and Gynecologists, was asked his opinion about the Sonoma Conference finding. He answered from the point of view of traditional moral and ethical standards by stating:

> The fact that seventeen of twenty expert panelists believe that some severely defective infants "should be killed under certain conditions"

... is not only deeply disturbing to our traditional concept of the inherent value of human life but is potentially shattering to the foundation of Western civilization.[8]

Dr. Schmidt concluded his remarks by saying:

Finally, the issue is clouded by questions raised as to what state of perfection or imperfection qualifies a human being as a person. The Supreme Court decision of 1973 has already severely limited this qualification. Under current law, the existence of every future member of our society may be terminated (within the uterus) according to the value judgment of one, or at the most two, private individuals. To extend this contingency of private value judgment to the newborn infant in either ethical standard or in the law would be another ominous step backward.[9]

Concerning a symposium on birth defects sponsored by the Medical Society of the District of Columbia, Dr. John A. Robertson of the University of Wisconsin Law School and Medical School spoke what seems to me a word of wisdom in bringing this kind of discussion down to earth. He said that "one must decide for whose benefit is the decision to withhold treatment from a child with severe birth defects. Is no life better than one of 'low quality'? The person to ask is an individual who has a disabling birth defect."[10]

I have recently written the script for, acted in, and narrated several documentary films, collectively entitled *Whatever Happened to the Human Race?*, that I have undertaken with Francis A. Schaeffer, an American-born theologian-philosopher who lives in Switzerland.[11] The second of these films is on the subject of infanticide. I think one of the most compelling scenes in any of the films is one held in my living room where four of my patients born with defects incompatible with life and who were operated upon by me on the first day or two of life were assembled with four other patients who had developed lethal problems in early childhood. They were not coached in any way concerning what answer they were to give to my questions. They were told we were making some documentary movies and were writing a book on the general topic of *Whatever Happened to the Human Race?* We allowed time for them to talk with each other for about an hour in order to feel comfortable before being asked to participate in the film.

The patients at the time ranged in age from eleven to thirty-three years. One patient had been born with a number of major congenital anomalies down the midline of his body requiring, up to then, thirty-seven operative procedures for correction. Another was born without an esophagus, requiring transplantation of the colon to replace that absent organ. Still another was born with a tumor of the tongue necessitating almost total amputation of that structure in a series of operations. The fourth youngster with congenital defects was born with no rectum, no innervation of the bladder, and with major defects of the esophagus.

The other four children all had tumors. One was a benign tumor of the bones of the face, which had required a number of operations for correction and we still had not achieved perfection. The other three had cancers of the adrenal gland, of the parotid gland, and of the uterus, respectively. There can be no doubt about how such young people feel concerning the joy of living, despite the time-consuming and usually painful medical and surgical procedures they have endured to correct birth defects or situations discovered in early childhood. Here are samples of their comments:

> Because the start was a little abnormal, it doesn't mean you're going to finish that way. I'm a normal, functioning human being, capable of doing anything anybody else can.

> At times it got very hard, but life is certainly worth living. I married a wonderful guy and I'm just so happy.

> At the beginning it was a little difficult going back to school after surgery, but then things started looking up, with a little perseverance and support. I am an anesthetist and I'm happily married. Things are going great for me.

> I really think that all my operations and all the things I had wrong with me were worth it, because I really enjoy life and I don't really let the things that are wrong with me bother me.

> If anything, I think I've had an added quality to my life—an appreciation of life. I look forward to every single morning.

> Most of the problems are what my parents went through with the surgery. I've now been teaching high school for eight years and it's a great joy.

> They spend millions of dollars to send men to the moon. I think they can spend any amount necessary to save someone's life. A human life is so important because it's a gift—not something you can give, so you really don't have the right to take it either.

> I really don't consider myself handicapped. Life is just worth living. What else can I say?[12]

In another part of the film we talk to a young man who is now a graduate student. He was a thalidomide baby, born without a left leg and without arms below the elbows. When we asked this young man what he thought about those who say that people born with such serious birth defects should be eliminated, this, in part, was his reply.

They don't really see that what they are talking about is murder. I know, when I was born, the first thing my dad said to my mom was that "this one needs our love more." An individual with a handicap needs our love and needs us to help him grow into the being that God has made him to be. They are advocating that we destroy these children before they're even given a chance to live and to conquer their handicaps.

I'm very glad to be alive. I live a full, meaningful life. I have many friends and many things that I want to do in life. I think the secret of living with a handicap is realizing who you are–that you are a human being, somebody who is very special–looking at the things that you *can* do in spite of your handicap, and maybe even through your handicap.[13]

Anxious to know in my own patients what perceptions parents had years after their encounter with a surgical procedure to save a handicapped newborn's life, a study was done on thirty-one families in which I personally had operated on a child more than fifteen years before for the correction of esophageal atresia.[14] When fifty-three parents were asked what type of overall effect the situation had on the family, only two said the effect was strong and negative. Seven said the effect was mild and negative, ten said it was strong and positive, and fourteen claimed the effect was mild and positive. Eighteen parents thought there was *no* impact on the family.

The handicapped newborn is a great risk in the thinking, not only of some pediatricians and neonatologists, but also with ethicists, nonmedical scientists, and even the church. In *Ethics in Newborn Intensive Care,* edited by Jonsen and Garland, this paragraph appears:

Seen in this way, the defective child is more "unwanted" than the unplanned child. Can we say because the child was born alive the balancing of lives that is permitted in *Roe v. Wade,* mother for child–is out of the question? Does not a failure to consider the trade-off condemn the parents as surely as the earlier refusal to consider abortion condemned the mother?[15]

Roe v. Wade was not the balancing of the mother's life against the child's life, but it is stated here as though that had been the thesis and that it is now accepted. Note who is condemned when abortion is not done– the mother. This is very much like the manner in which the situational ethicist, Joseph Fletcher, leads his audience down the garden path. This is what he said in his 1973 discussion of death with dignity in the *American Journal of Nursing.*

It is ridiculous to give ethical approval to the positive ending of sub-human life in utero, as we do now in therapeutic abortions for reasons of mercy and compassion, but refuse to approve of positively ending a subhuman life in extremis. If we are morally obliged to put an end to a pregnancy when an amniocentesis reveals a terribly defective fetus, we are equally obliged to put an end to a patient's hopeless misery when a brain scan reveals that a patient with cancer has advanced brain metastases.[16]

Fletcher declares without a discussion that ethical approval has been given to the ending of the lives of babies out of compassion when you and I know that most of the unborn babies are destroyed at the whim and for the convenience of their mothers. Then Fletcher puts that nonexistent moral approval in the form of an obligation and says that because we are obliged to do that, we are also morally obliged to put the end to the life of a patient who has cancer with advanced brain metastases. He has declared the child with a congenital defect to be subhuman and then he declares the person at the end of life to be subhuman. "To argue otherwise," he says, "is ridiculous."[17]

Two Nobel laureates have voiced opinions concerning this subject of infanticide, although they did not include that word in their statements. In May 1973 James Watson, of DNA double helix fame, stated:

If a child were not declared alive until three days after birth, then all parents could be allowed the choice only a few are given under the present system. The doctor could allow the child to die if the parents so choose and save a lot of misery and suffering. I believe this view is the only rational, compassionate attitude to have.[18]

In January 1978 Francis Crick, also a Nobel Laureate, was quoted in the *Pacific News Service* as saying: "No newborn infant should be declared human until it has passed certain tests regarding its genetic endowment and that if it fails these tests, it forfeits the right to live."[19]

If any group of physicians knows what can be accomplished by surgery on the handicapped newborn—and the proper support of the patient and his family in subsequent years—it is pediatric surgeons. Drs. Anthony Shaw, Judson G. Randolph, and Barbara Manard surveyed members of the surgical section of the American Academy of Pediatrics in reference to the management of newborns with handicaps.[20] Of the 400 pediatric surgeons queried, 267 (67 percent) completed questionnaires. A separate group of 308 pediatricians completed 190 questionnaires (62 percent). The first question was, "Do you believe that the life of each and every newborn infant should be saved if it is within our ability to do so?" Eighty percent of those surgeons with my kind of background answered no.[21]

Here are some other readily remembered statistics. Seventy-six percent of the pediatric surgeons would acquiesce in the parents' decision to refuse consent for surgery in a newborn with intestinal obstruction if the infant also had Down's syndrome, or mongolism.[22] An almost unbelievable fact is that 8 percent of the surgeons (respondents) said they would acquiesce to the parents' wishes if the child had nothing other than simple intestinal atresia, the operation which is almost 100 percent successful and life after which is completely normal.[23]

To return to the infant with duodenal obstruction, which is fatal but easily correctable, and Down's syndrome, the following percentages are significant. Twenty-three percent of the pediatric surgeons group would move the parents in the direction of not signing a consent for surgery and an operative permit making it the physician's decision whether or not to let the baby die; nevertheless, if the family desired surgery the surgeon would perform it.[24] Over half of the same group said they would provide the parents with all known facts and make the decision completely the parents'. (Surely the bias of the doctor would show through.) Only 16 percent would try to persuade the parents to allow surgery but would not take them to court on refusal. Three percent would get a court order if the parents refused consent for operation.[25]

The schizophrenic nature of these replies is indicated by the fact that if they acquiesce to the parents' decision to withhold lifesaving surgery 63 percent would have stopped all supportive treatment, 30 percent would have given oral feedings which of course would be vomited immediately, but less than .05 percent would have terminated the infant's life by an injection of a drug such as morphine.[26]

Dr. J. Alex Haller, the surgeon who participated in the Kennedy Foundation film *Who Shall Survive?,* reasons this way:

Should every life be protected and cared for? Have advances in amniocentesis and intrauterine diagnosis brought with them the moral question of interfering with a viable human being while it is in the womb? We asked parents to make the decision at this stage.[27]

Haller recognizes he is dealing with a viable human and that the question of interference is a moral one, but then he also acknowledges that he asks parents to make the decision about whether or not to let the baby be born. Dr. Haller continues: "Then the baby is born. Does the responsibility for the decision change hands? Does coming out of the uterus make the difference?" Haller's reasoning based on his first premise is right thus far. Why could he not ask, "Does achieving the age of five years make any difference—or ten years, or fifteen years, or twenty-five?"

There is a disturbing trend that I would like to mention—the process of "selection," as it is called in England. Spina bifida is one of the most common congenital malformations but it is far more common in the British Isles than it is in the United States. Patients' parents are led to believe that when a child is born with spina bifida, a surgeon operates on the child and he gets well, or one does not operate and the child dies. This is not the case; spina bifida of itself is not a lethal lesion. However, it is now the custom in England to operate only upon those children who have good legs, good rectums, good bladders, et cetera. This is known as the process of selection. They joke about putting the other patients on a low calorie diet, which means starving them to death. About 25 percent are operated upon and 75 percent are selected to die. The technique is to oversedate them with chloral hydrate or phenobarbital. They become so floppy they cannot take their feedings and die of dehydration and starvation. Occasional patients who do not become sedated enough under this regimen are given increasing doses of morphine for nonexistent pain.[28]

Such performance in England is serious enough. More serious is the obvious shift from terminating infants with lethal (although correctable) lesions to terminating infants with both lethal and *non*lethal lesions. It takes very little time for a so-called "social advance" to cross the Atlantic to America. It took abortion-on-demand only six years.

I recently talked to about 7,000 people in several cities in England while showing the *Whatever Happened to the Human Race?* films. In Birmingham, after presentation of our film on infanticide, and after Professor Zachary (as outspoken in his country as I am in mine) had talked on infanticide, a woman rose to ask a question.

> I am a general practitioner in the National Health Service. Three years ago a daughter was born to us who had spina bifida and I was told that she would die within three weeks. When a nurse told me that our daughter was being starved to death, I signed her out of the hospital against advice. She is now a bright, adorable three-year-old girl who is the light of our lives. However, she has an incontinent bladder and orthopedic deformities which keep her from walking. But because I signed her out of the hospital against advice and because she was initially classified as nontreatable, there is no way that I can obtain any urologic or orthopedic help for my child. At my own expense I am keeping her on urinary antibiotics in order to protect her kidneys. What can I do?

Professor Zachary told her that the only recourse in England was to seek private care. I told her that if she could get the child to Philadelphia we would eventually send her home walking in calipers, her urine controlled with an ileal bladder—and she might even be the second lady prime minister of Great Britain some day.

Semantics play such a role in the lack of consensus concerning abortion that I must mention a most disturbing semantic change in referring to the newborn. Inasmuch as the 1973 Supreme Court decision has deprived the fetus of hitherto well-established rights as a person, a semantic change descriptive of the handicapped newborn has in the minds of many removed the responsibility for infanticide by referring to the handicapped newborn as *fetus-ex-utero.*

Even segments of the church have been outspoken on the subject of infanticide. The task force of The Anglican Church of Canada in 1977 concluded that it was morally right to terminate the lives of newborn infants with severe brain damage. The callousness of the report is evident in its phraseology.

> Our sense and emotion lead us to the grave mistake of treating human looking shapes as if they were human, although they lack the least vestige of human behavior and intellect. In fact the only way to treat such defective infants humanely is not to treat them as human.[29]

The eleven people who made that statement had backgrounds in medicine, nursing, law, and theology. Happily, the General Synod of The Anglican Church of Canada did not approve the report; but the fact that such a report came forth from an official group of a major denomination says much about the direction taken by some church people in regard to infanticide.

In any discussion of the rights and wrongs of euthanasia (do not forget that infanticide is also euthanasia—euthanasia reserved for infants), one always gets around to a discussion of whether it is fitting and proper to withhold extraordinary care from a patient known to have a limited life expectancy. In dealing with the newborn it is never possible to talk about extraordinary care. Not only is it difficult to define what was extraordinary yesterday is ordinary today, it is fact that all of the patients I operate on in the newborn period would not survive were it not for the exercise of the most extraordinary care and the most advanced technology available to modern medical science. Yet the great majority of patients I operate on not only are restored to life, but to good life, and to long life.

I practice medicine in the realm of trust between my patient's family and me. I do withhold treatment from patients under certain circumstances, but if I do, I have to know three things: an extraordinary amount about the disease process in question, an extraordinary amount about my patient, and an extraordinary amount about the relationship of my patient to the disease process in question. If I do not know all of these three, then I must, as an ethical physician, in any decision process come down on the side of life.

I think there is an innate understanding, in the physician whose profession and art is a calling, that does not make it necessary for him to enunciate guidelines (such as I have just mentioned) or to have rules that he must live by. If I had to make a statement concerning rules, it would be this: I give every patient all of the life to which I think he is entitled but I do not prolong his process of dying. Now, in reference to the handicapped newborn, it could be safely said that, unattended, all of my patients are dying when I meet them. The difference between these handicapped neonates and, say, a child dying of cancer at seven years, is that well-established surgical procedures exist for the management of the neonate which will save his life and put him back into society for a full life span, while the options for treatment of the dying cancer patient are all palliative at best.

It is common parlance now to talk about the "bottom line," and I guess the bottom line for most people is an economic one. Such is very often the case when we are talking about the care of handicapped infants. The discussion of economics when it comes to saving a human life is abhorrent to me because I have never been able to put a price on a human life. I can honestly say that, in the thirty-five years I have been involved with the care of children, I have never felt that I was in a situation of finite medical resources. When I was short a bed, I could find one in an equivalent institution. When I was short of respirators, I could rent a spare. Whenever I needed extra hours of surgical, anesthetic, or nursing support, I could always find an individual willing to go the extra mile. Never forget that the first time anything is done, it is extraordinarily expensive in comparison to what the cost will be down the line of experience. Let me give you a superb example of how the most extraordinary care delivered to a handicapped newborn child with no possible hope for recovery has opened the door to the salvage of innumerable subsequent patients and the improvement of care for many more.

A number of years ago a newborn child was operated on in the Children's Hospital of Philadelphia. Almost her entire bowel was found to be gangrenous and the unaffected segment was not long enough to support life.[30] In an institution whose personnel were aggressively seeking innovative procedures and trying desperately to push back the frontiers of pediatric surgery, one of my colleagues resected the gangrenous bowel and kept the child alive on total parenteral nutrition. The hope was that a small bowel transplant would eventually be possible to restore this child to a satisfactory existence. Before that technique could be achieved the patient succumbed—but not until she had been on total parenteral nutrition, gaining weight and developing according to acceptable standards, over a period of 400 days. The cost was enormous and the patient died, but because she was the first ever to be maintained on total parenteral nutrition, medical science learned a great proportion of what it now knows about hyperalimentation or total parenteral nutrition. Although this little girl died, the experience gained with her, which was intentionally for her own good and not the good of society, did provide society with a now-recognized nutritional technique that has saved the lives of millions of children and hundreds of thousands of adults throughout the world. In addition to that, hospital stays have been shortened, wounds have healed more quickly, and rehabilitation has been possible sooner (all with great savings in dollars), and hitherto almost unmanageable situations, like small intestinal fistulae, have come under surgical control.

In a November 1979 issue of *The Lancet,* under a department designated *Points of View,* an article appeared entitled "Nontreatment of Defective

Newborn Babies."[31] This is the only anonymous medical article I have ever seen published. The author identifies himself as a pediatrician drawing cases from a population of 450,000 over a period of fifteen years and says he is a Christian. This unknown author states:

> The question often occurs to me when talking to parents of a newborn baby with a severe handicap, what I would answer if the child when he came of age should ask me, "Why did you let me live?" My possible answers, legality, my lack of courage, sound hollow. I could certainly not plead ignorance. The only answer which I could find morally defensible would be, "Your parents believed they could bring you up to be emotionally whole, though physically crippled."[32]

That I would call in the vernacular a "cop-out." I see many physically normal adults today who are emotionally crippled while physically whole. Will they be next on the list for extermination?

Let me match credentials with the author. I have been practicing pediatric surgery longer than any person in the United States and Canada who is now in the field. Because of the scarcity of pediatric surgeons in the early days of the practice of this specialty, my early experience came from patients who traveled extraordinary distances. I therefore can say, I think with some degree of certainty, that no one in the United States and Canada has operated on more babies with congenital defects. I can also say, without exception, that I have never had a parent come to me in later years and say, "Why did you try so hard to save the life of my child?" Nor have I ever had a grown child come to me and say, "Why did you try so hard to save my life when I was born?" Some of the patients I operated on on the first day of life are now 36 years old.

More than that, as I have become increasingly interested in this subject over the years, I do not now wait to see if parents will come to me but I go to them and say, "Just in the quiet of this room and between us, are you sorry I worked so hard to save your child's life?" No one has ever said "Yes." Many wish things could have been smoother, but none have preferred a dead child. I have a remarkable rapport with a number of the patients I operated on years ago and they uniformly joke with me about their handicaps. None wishes to be dead. None of those patients have committed suicide.

I would like to suggest to you some of the things that happen in this country in reference to the handicapped newborn and his family. First of all, they encounter one of four kinds of physicians. One physician will act in support of the child and family as I have suggested that my colleagues and I do. Another physician will present death as an option in management. A third will suggest institutionalization for the diagnosis in question, and the fourth is one of the previous two who becomes hostile toward the family because his advice has not been taken.

What of the parents? They have several options open to them. If they are not in the hands of a team that will do all that it can to bring the pertinent agencies into contact with the family for their ultimate benefit, they will have to forage for themselves. These parents seek on their own what society has to offer; and, on occasion, when they find society's effort to be less than adequate, they either restructure the lives of their family to fit the inadequate provisions, or they attempt to be innovative enough to start in motion supportive services that will benefit not only their child but others with similar problems.

This reaction of families has been clearly documented by Rosalyn Benjamin Darling in a study she did on twenty-five intact families who were raising a child with spina bifida. It is appropriate that the title of her excellent book is *Families Against Society*.[33]

What are the positions of the physicians? I think Rosalyn Darling accurately answers that question in her summary of the in-depth interviews she had with fifteen pediatricians who were caring for spina bifida patients being raised in intact families. She observes:

As the parents' data indicated, their greatest interactional difficulties involved physicians and other medical personnel. The two areas of greatest conflict were: (1) the situation of first information—most parents were dissatisfied with the manner in which they were told about their children's problems, particularly with the hesitancy of doctors to tell the truth, and (2) the willingness to treat—many parents complained about doctors who did not seem to enjoy treating handicapped children in their everyday practices and who, as a result, treated such children in a less than human manner and treated their parents in a blaming way, especially if they refused institutionalization for their children.[34]

What Dr. Darling is describing here is the pediatrician's assessment of the quality of life he projects for the infant born with an anomaly. He underestimates the love and devotion already present in the parents of the disabled child and therefore fails to realize that institutionalization will not provide the ready answer for the parents that it might provide for him.

It is my hope that in my present and future pursuits I can be instrumental in the creation of a comprehensive service to be made available to concerned physicians and parents to take the sting out of managing a handicapped child. What I envision is a national computer data-bank type service that physicians or parents can tap by telephone to obtain up-to-date diagnostic information, locations of the most competent local diagnostic services, locations of closest competent therapeutic services, locations of available governmental and private agencies that could be of help to parents and children, and listings of nearby parents who have coped with similar problems in the past. If this service can be made available to parents and physicians alike, I think the terrible fear that the odds against the handicapped child and his family are too great to make any effort worthwhile can be removed.

We are constantly bombarded by propaganda concerning the cost of the handicapped to society. I submit that the costs imposed upon our society by all of the physically handicapped, and by all of the mentally handicapped – today and in the future – are and will be but a drop in the bucket compared to the costs imposed by the morally handicapped. I have never read anything in the newspapers about how the physically handicapped have perpetrated tremendous crimes against society. The same could be said about the mentally handicapped. But newspaper headlines and commentaries in news magazines constantly remind us that we are burdened almost beyond our ability to stand it with the cost of the morally handicapped. These are the people who perpetrate our crimes and kill our citizens. These are the people for whom we are asked to provide every conceivable rehabilitation program. We are asked to see that they have easy sentences when convicted. We are informed about the advantages of plea bargaining and for some of them there is not even an ultimate penalty because capital punishment has been abolished. Why then do we demand perfection for those who have physical and mental handicaps while we go to great lengths to tolerate, and protect, gross imperfection from that much larger number who are morally handicapped?

* * *

In summary, I submit that once abortion-on-demand is accepted by the medical profession as a means of solving social problems, it is easy to move from there to the concept of the handicapped newborn as being a *fetus-ex-utero*. Even if one does not use that term, one can refer to his life as having only "potential," or that he does not have "life in the real sense," or "meaningful personhood." All this can be summed up by saying that there is such a thing as "life not worthy to be lived," a concept that Leo Alexander, the American psychiatrist at the Nuremburg trials, affirms to be the beginning of all the Nazi atrocities that made the Nuremburg trials a necessity.[35] With the door open to this much, the attitude of society is easily swayed to believe that not only can the child with a defect not cope with it and have a satisfactory life, but that his mere presence is a source of great hardship to his parents, his siblings, and society in general.

The profession of medicine, having tolerated the changes in approach to the patient already mentioned, has been able to share with the parents the responsibility for the destruction of a child without, I believe, much concern about the eventual and possibly overwhelming guilt these parents will feel in days to come when they realize that they have opted to kill their child. Semantics have made infanticide palatable by never referring to the practice by that word, but by using such euphemisms as "selection."

"Starving a child to death" becomes "allowing him to die." Although infanticide is not talked about even in professional circles, the euphemisms are. It is all illegal, but the law has turned its back. The day will come when the argument will be as it was for abortion: "Let's legalize what is already happening." Then what is legal is right. Attention will then be turned to the next class of individuals that might be exterminated without too loud an outcry.

When a hospital is geared to save lives at any cost, this attitude affects health care down to the most mundane level. On the other hand, if one set of patients can be eliminated at will, the whole spirit of struggling to save lives is lost, and it is not long before a doctor or nurse will say: "Why try so hard on anybody? After all, we deliberately fail to treat some patients and we actually kill others." Even if not expressed this blatantly, a moral erosion will take place that will ultimately undermine the care of *all* patients in an institution that can find an ethical reason to kill a patient placed in its care.

Notes

1. REPORT OF THE JOSEPH P. KENNEDY FOUNDATION INT'L SYMPOSIUM ON HUMAN RIGHTS, RETARDATION AND RESEARCH, Oct. 16, 1971. For an extended version of the Johns Hopkins case study, *see* Gustafson, *Mongolism, Parental Desires and the Right to Life,* 16 PERSPECTIVES IN BIOLOGY & MED. 529 (1973).

2. Duff & Campbell, *Moral and Ethical Dilemmas In The Special-Care Nursery,* 289 NEW ENG. J. MED. 890 (1973).

3. *Id.* at 890.

4. *Id.* at 891.

5. 290 NEW ENGLAND J. MED. 518 (1974).

6. *Id.*

7. Vaughan, *MD-Parent Decision Needed to Kill Infant,* PEDIATRIC NEWS, April, 1977, at 30.

8. Schmidt, *Panelists' Views on Killing Infant: 'Threat to Western Civilization,'* PEDIATRIC NEWS, April, 1977, at 32.

9. *Id.*

10. PEDIATRIC NEWS, March, 1977, at 4.

11. F. SCHAEFFER & C. E. KOOP, WHATEVER HAPPENED TO THE HUMAN RACE? (1979).

12. *Id.* at 64–65.

13. *Id.* at 65.

14. Koop et al., *The Social, Psychological and Economic Problems of the Patient's Family After Secondary Repair of Esophegeal Atresia,* 17 KINDERCHIRURGIE (Supp. July, 1975).

15. Marks, *The Defective Newborn: An Analytic Framework for a Policy Dialog,* in ETHICS OF NEWBORN INTENSIVE CARE 97, 106 (A. Jonsen & M. Garland, eds. 1976).

16. Fletcher, *Ethics and Euthanasia,* 73 AM. J. NURSING 670, 673 (1973).

17. *Id.*

18. TIME, May 28, 1973, at 104.

19. *See* SCHAEFFER & KOOP, *supra* note 11, at 73.

20. Shaw, Randolph, & Manard, *Ethical Issues in Pediatrics Surgery: A National Survey of Pediatricians and Pediatric Surgeons,* 60 PEDIATRICS 588 (1977).

21. *Id.* at 589. Of 259 responses from pediatric surgeons, 17 percent said yes and 83 percent said no. "Because the respondents [were] not a random sample of either [pediatric surgeons or pediatricians] but represented self-selected subgroups of entire populations, the use of inferential statistics is inappropriate." *Id.*

22. *Id.* at 590. Fifty percent of the pediatricians' group responded that they would acquiesce in such a decision.

23. *Id.* at 590–91. The authors note, however, that these respondents' answers to other questions indicated that most had read the question too hastily. These physicians were not more likely than others to refuse to operate on a baby with Down's syndrome. *Id.* at 591.

24. *Id.* at 591–92.

25. *Id.* Several of those who responded checked more than one option. (The pediatric surgeons usually chose to move the parents in the direction of not signing, and also to provide the parents with information and make the decision completely theirs.)

26. *Id.* at 592–93. It is interesting to note the difference between the responses of the pediatric surgeons and the pediatricians. Generally, the pediatricians were more willing to attempt to save the infant's life.

27. *See* sources cited at note 1, *supra.*

28. *See generally,* " 'Black Day' for Handicapped," HUMANITY, Dec. 1981 (on file with editors).

29. ANGLICAN CHURCH OF CANADA, TASK FORCE ON HUMAN LIFE, INTERIM REPORT, *Dying: Considerations Concerning the Passage from Life to Death* (presented to a General Synod, Aug. 11–18, 1977). *See* N.Y. Times, July 28, 1977.

30. Wilmore, Groff, Bishop, & Dubrick, *Total Parenteral Nutrition in Infants With Catastrophic Gastrointestinal Anomalies,* 4 J. PEDIATRIC SURGERY 181 (1969).

31. LANCET, Nov. 24, 1979, at 1123.

32. *Id.*

33. R. B. DARLING, FAMILIES AGAINST SOCIETY: REACTIONS TO CHILDREN WITH BIRTH DEFECTS (1979).

34. *Id.* at 78.

35. Alexander, *Medical Science Under Dictatorship,* 241 NEW ENGLAND J. MED. 39 (1949).

9
Ethical Reflections on Infanticide

Arthur J. Dyck

Students laugh when they learn that a physician once considered all human beings in the care of physicians as living question marks. It is no exaggeration today, however, that newborn infants with handicaps are living question marks—not necessarily due to their physical defects, but due to the philosophy of a growing number of health professionals that such infants should not necessarily receive comfort, and comforting (or lifesaving) therapeutic interventions.

That handicapped infants are at risk due to that philosophy is glaringly dramatized in *Who Shall Live?*, the documentary film portraying the death (at Johns Hopkins Hospital) of a child born with both Down's syndrome and duodenal atresia, which death was allowed by the child's physician when the parents refused consent for the treatment of the atresia. Obviously the child's physician was of the opinion that the child's right to treatment (which in this case was the child's right to life) was less than his parents' right to leave him to die, and apparently the physician's opinion (or philosophy) was not challenged at the time by the hospital administration and any number of health professionals aware of the decision.

In the currently at large debate over the Johns Hopkins case, and other cases like it that have occurred since, some argue that such infants should be left to die; others argue that such infants should be treated. Disagreement exists also about who is to make such decisions. Some contend that parents should decide such cases; others that physicians should; still others that the courts should—or the courts should at least decide the locus of authority for making such decisions.

A basic moral value is at stake here: life and justice in the form of equitable treatment, and otherwise doing no harm. If we wish to uphold life as

Arthur J. Dyck received his B.A. from Tabor College, his M.A. in psychology and philosophy from the University of Kansas, and his Ph.D. in religious ethics from Harvard. He is the Mary B. Saltonstall Professor of Population Ethics, Harvard School of Public Health and Harvard Divinity School. He has written extensively on the ethics of termination of medical treatment, including coediting the book *Ethics in Medicine.*

a human right worthy of legal protection and if we wish to uphold fair treatment, including equal protection and due process before the law, what would and should guide us in making medical decisions regarding handicapped newborns and incompetents generally? Paul Ramsey has suggested an excellent resolution of the debate.[1] The ethical rule of practice should be to ask of the medical treatment being contemplated: (1) Is it offered to normal adult patients? (2) Is it given to normal patients who, because of age, cannot themselves refuse treatment? and, (3) Is it protected in such patients by law against any private decision to withhold it?

Ramsey is presupposing that normal adult patients will be offered treatment designed to improve their conditions, in some instances treatment necessary to save life or relieve pain or suffering. He is presupposing also that similar treatment will be given to those who are otherwise normal and who, because of age, are not able or allowed as newborns or minors to refuse the treatment given. Furthermore, Ramsey is presupposing that treatment deemed necessary and efficacious to save life, or diminish pain or suffering, is legally supported; that courts will not generally permit anyone, whether medical professionals or parents, to withhold such treatment from those who cannot ask for or refuse it. In short, Ramsey's presumption is that all human beings have a right to life and to equal protection of that right. Failure to remove a life-threatening blockage in a patient's intestine constitutes a failure to realize the patient's right to life, and failure to do the same for a newborn because it is a newborn, or because it is judged to lack certain normal mental or physical capacities, constitutes a failure to realize that newborn's right to equal protection of its right to life.

It is clear that some disagree with the philosophy underlying Ramsey's suggested solution. Neither present medical practice nor court decisions consistently conform to the rule of practice he has enunciated. Why is this so? What understanding of rights to life and justice is behind this? How can and how should these rights be understood and realized? Any adequate response to these questions requires us to take up three distinct but related developments in thought and medical decisions: (1) confusion over letting die and killing; (2) controversy over who should make medical decisions for incompetents; and (3) conceptions of personhood.

If a newborn, handicapped or not, is considered to be dying, some would say ordinary care is called for but not extraordinary. Adults who are dying have the right to refuse such care for themselves while receiving comfort and pain relief, even life-shortening pain relief. Pain relief that may shorten life is not done with the intention of hastening death. The double effect argument applies here. Allowing the dying to die without heroic efforts to prolong every moment of the dying process has been called "allowing to die" and distinguished morally from "killing."

But, recently, some have argued that there is no morally justifiable distinction between allowing to die and directly inducing death, and that if one can justify the former, as health professionals generally can, one can justify the latter. James Rachels has recently argued this quite forcefully.[2] To make his case that any effort to shorten life, or any failure to prolong life (that is, "allowing to die") is akin to killing, Rachels offers the following examples:

> Smith stands to gain a large inheritance if anything should happen to his six-year-old cousin. One evening while the child is taking his bath, Smith sneaks into the bathroom, drowns the child, and then arranges things so that it will look like an accident.
>
> Jones also stands to gain if anything should happen to his six-year-old cousin. Like Smith, Jones sneaks in planning to drown the child in his bath. However, just as he enters the bathroom, Jones sees the child slip, hit his head, and fall face down in the water. Jones is delighted; he stands by, ready to push the child's head back under if it is necessary, but it is not necessary. With only a little thrashing about, the child drowns all by himself, "accidentally," as Jones watches and does nothing.[3]

From these examples, Rachels argues that Smith killed the child whereas Jones allowed the child to die. That is the only difference between them. But is there any *moral* difference between killing and letting die in these two instances? Did not both men desire and achieve the same end when they acted or failed to act?

The examples cited by Rachels parallel certain cases in which the distinction between allowing to die and killing has indeed eroded within the medical profession. In instances in which physicians have decided, with concurrence of parents, not to save the lives of certain infants whose lives could be saved but who are diagnosed as having some irreversible handicap that would not be ameliorated by lifesaving interventions, Rachels is right when he argues that there is no moral difference between these particular instances of allowing to die and directly taking life. In fact, Rachels understandably points out that the device of not feeding these infants and letting them linger, as in the Johns Hopkins case, is less merciful than the direct inducement of death. However, is it not also possible to argue that it is as morally wrong to let those die who can be saved as it is directly to kill them, while at the same time arguing consistently that there are instances of allowing to die which are morally justified?

To understand the situation of the imminently dying, as well as the situation of health professionals responsible for their care, requires that we look at illustrations common in medicine yet not covered by Rachels.

Imagine that Mr. Brown has fallen on a small rocky ledge in the midst of rising floodwaters. The area is quite inaccessible; it would take days to summon help, and the floodwaters will inevitably rise over him and sweep him down a steep waterfall well before help could be summoned and brought back. Nor can he be rescued from the shore even though it is close enough to allow Brown to converse with someone on the shore. Imagine, also, that Brown has been injured from the fall and is lying on jagged rocks in intense pain.

In the first scenario, Mr. Green is on the shore. He is an expert marksman and has a loaded pellet rifle such as those used in "Wild Kingdom." If Brown were shot with them, he would be rendered painlessly asleep until the floodwaters drowned him. Thus, Green has powers and skills relative to Brown that are comparable to those health professionals have relative to the imminently, irreversibly dying. Why might one consider using pellets rather than lethal bullets? Well, as in virtually all cases of individuals judged to be dying, there is some chance, however slight, that Brown will be rescued. For example, a helicopter pilot might fly over the floodwaters, see Brown, and put out a ladder that allows someone to descend and rescue him. If Green deliberately shoots Brown with bullets intended to kill him and succeeds, Green is morally and legally responsible for the death of Brown, not the floodwaters. If, however, Green intentionally sedates Brown with pellets, there is no way he can be held morally and legally culpable for Brown's death. Similarly, if Green does nothing, simply letting Brown die with no consideration of his pain or suffering, he cannot be charged with Brown's death. Letting die in such circumstances is not akin to killing. Many may see Green as cruel, if he fails to use the nonlethal pain relief available to him, but they will not see him as a murderer.

Now, suppose Green finds a rope, too short for Green to pull Brown up, but long enough that if dropped to Brown, Brown could hoist himself from the jagged rocks onto which he has fallen to a nearby small grassy spot. If the grassy spot were above Brown, in addition to possible relief of his pain, his life would be lengthened slightly because of his being further above the rising water. But if the grassy spot is below the rocks he is on, Green's dropping the rope to Brown so that he can lower himself may hasten Brown's death. If Green therefore supplies the short rope and Brown lowers himself to the grassy spot, Green will be a party to Brown's shortening his own life for the sake of being more comfortable. Let us posit that Green drops the rope to Brown after carefully scanning the sky and land for any imminent sources of rescue. Is Green now responsible for the death of Brown? No. But what if one argues that he is an accomplice to the shortening of Brown's life? Is that morally tantamount to killing Brown?

The reason we would not accuse Green of killing Brown—even though by providing him some means to be more comfortable Green has thereby shortened Brown's potential life span—is that other considerations enter into the choices we make with regard to how long we will live. For example, we decide to work hard. This decision could shorten our lives. If, however, our work is important and justified on various grounds, and if, as is usually the case, we cannot be certain of the direct effect of this work on the shortening of our lives, we do not consider it a decision to commit suicide. Similarly, we permit vacations. Vacations may contribute to health. Yet, some vacations expose us to risks to life and health. Even so, we would not generally attempt to deny people vacations to ski or climb mountains on moral grounds, unless, perhaps, we knew such people to be careless. Why, then, would we deem it morally unjustified for this struggling, imminently dying man out on a rock to ease his pain by lowering himself to a more comfortable position for his last hours? Dying persons may not wish to have their lives shortened in order to be made more comfortable, but if they do, there is nothing morally reprehensible about requesting what amounts to a vacation from pain and discomfort. Both Brown and Green are making a decision about how to live while dying.

Now, imagine that Mr. Brown is incompetent, whether as an adult or as an infant, normal or handicapped. Ramsey's rule of practice would sanction, morally and legally, the various interventions open to Green, except shooting Brown to death. Doing nothing or walking off would be regarded as morally unjustified, given comparable possibilities to relieve pain and suffering. But, notice that so far no desire to die has been imputed to Brown. What about the situation in which Brown asks that he be killed? Despite the success Cicely Saunders and others have had in treating dying patients, and nurturing in them their desire to live, thereby warding off their desire to be killed,[4] there are those who contend that they will have a genuine desire to be killed should certain circumstances arise. Most often, they anticipate a wish to be killed not because they are dying, but rather because they are in a condition, dying or not, they consider to be intolerable. The condition considered to be the most intolerable is irreversible loss of consciousness or cognition. Those who would wish to be killed in such a condition would probably ask that their deaths be induced immediately and painlessly. Where speed and certainty is insisted upon, direct action by others is the surest and, hence, most merciful. If one assumes, then, that some individuals will have a medical condition in which they will prefer a swift, painless death to any continuation of life, what should be done for . . . and, hence, . . . incompetents is problematic indeed. Does this incompetent adult, minor, or infant wish to live? How can one know? And, if it is sometimes merciful to kill the incompetent, on what grounds do we deny the request of a competent adult who is convinced that killing would be the most merciful thing we could do for him? Everyone, so one argument goes, has a right to die. Thus, a moral obligation would exist to secure and protect that right. And, some would add, the law ought to enforce it.[5] If this philosophy is pervasive enough, Ramsey's rule of practice has no predictable hold on individual, medical, and legal practices. That appears to be our present situation.

The decision of the U.S. Supreme Court on abortion in *Roe v. Wade* provides the model many would urge us to follow in the care of the incompetent adult and newly born. An act that is unjustified killing for some citizens can be permitted: (1) if the entity being killed has no legal standing; and (2) if those deciding whether or not to kill the individual in question have a right to privacy, protected by law, a right that allows them to decide whether the taking of life is morally right or wrong, and allows them to decide whether who is killed should or should not have legal standing. The decision as to whether a handicapped incompetent dies or is treated then becomes a decision for physicians, parents, next of kin, or legal guardians.

Picture a steep ravine with a ledge halfway down the side. Green is a skilled climber and guide who has often descended into the ravine to rescue individuals who have fallen. No stranger to the ravine who fell to that ledge would be able to find the only way out in time to avoid starving to death. And only a skilled climber with proper equipment could negotiate the climb once the route was found. In this hypothetical case a baby Brown has accidentally fallen to that ledge. Baby Brown is (or promises to be) handicapped. We know that some would urge rescue in such cases and some would urge against it. The reasons are varied, but many individuals—and courts—would settle the issue by deciding whose *right to privacy* is to be involved. That is, they would decide by deciding who will decide.

How does that work? Some insist that the decision whether to rescue a baby Brown should be made by Green, that is, by someone with appropriate skills and experience in rescuing individuals from that ledge and who has had to deal with the sorrow or joy or both that follows reunion of the infant and its parents or guardians.[6] Who else, some contend, can assess the risks and the worth of the enterprise for all concerned? Among those who support the primary authority of Green, some would insist that he rescue the infant and persuade the Browns to accept that. Others would contend that judgments have to be made about the worth of such a baby, so that Green would sometimes perform the rescue, sometimes not. Some would not save such a baby at risk of retardation in certain severe cases of spina bifida.[7] Others would insist that all cases of spina bifida be aided.[8]

Many parents, medical professionals, and lawyers generally presume that parents have and should have the final authority in making decisions regarding the well-being of infants and minor dependents. Where parents are making these decisions about when and whether a baby such as Brown is to be kept alive, they differ in the same way evidenced by the Greens, the experts at lifesaving. When you are a baby Brown, your life depends upon who your parents are if they are in charge, or on who the expert climbers are when they are in charge.

Sometimes, where parents or guardians have not allowed experts to rescue baby Brown, the cases have been brought to court. In the past the courts most often have decided what Ramsey would have them decide: that baby Brown's life should be saved, protests from whatever quarter notwithstanding.[9] As in *Roe v. Wade,* however, courts presently are more concerned with protecting an individual right to privacy, designating who has it, and making a judgment as to how it will best be realized. In this atmosphere, what will happen to an irreversibly handicapped infant, child, adult—or adult incompetent—cannot be predicted. If a court, and the medical practitioners under its jurisdiction, follow the reasoning of the New Jersey Supreme Court regarding Karen Ann Quinlan,[10] this is what we should expect: Green and the parents or legal guardians are authorized to refuse to rescue baby Brown whenever health professionals chosen by the guardians, and a hospital ethics committee, concur that baby Brown is irreversibly comatose and will allegedly never again attain a cognitive or sapient state. (The term "sapience" is hard to pin down, but it is some kind of higher cortical function associated with sentience or consciousness.) Apparently, the age of the patient does not matter—nor does it matter whether or not the patient is dying. Karen Ann Quinlan was not a minor and not clearly dying. What is to be protected in cases such as hers is the patient's right (to privacy) to refuse treatment. The parent or a designated legal guardian is the one to carry out that right. Potentially, a wide range of cases could fall under the Quinlan decision.

If a court follows the highest court of Massachusetts, the right to privacy of incompetents is not ultimately under a parent's jurisdiction. In the Saikewicz decision, the right to privacy, which includes a right to refuse lifesaving treatment, is explicitly a substitute judgment made on behalf of incompetent patients by the court.[11] Again, this would be true for any incompetent of any age whose life or comfort is threatened by treatment or the lack thereof. Ironically, the Massachusetts court said that the quality of life should not count in such a judgment, and yet they ruled that Saikewicz should not be treated because, as one who was retarded, he would not wish or understand the pain or discomfort of the treatment for leukemia. They made this quality-of-life judgment on his behalf, even though most competent patients normally choose treatment. The kinds of decisions that follow from Saikewicz will vary (and have varied) considerably. Even the same case is variously judged. In the Chad Green case, a child with leukemia, the courts ordered treatment over the objections of the parents, then ordered no treatment, and finally returned to demanding treatment. At that point, the parents left the country and eventually Chad Green ended this sad story by dying. What might have been is hard to say, although present leukemia treatment in Massachusetts apparently leads to remission for 50 percent or more in cases such as Chad Green's.

The point is that minors, the handicapped, or possibly other incompetents—like the fetus—may not have legal status as persons and as bearers of rights.[12] Recently, the New Jersey Supreme Court held that a retarded child had no constitutional right to free education in New Jersey, even though that constitution explicitly states that every child between the ages of five and nineteen is entitled to free, public education.[13] In effect, the New Jersey Court regards retarded minors as something other than, or less than, children—in direct violation of the constitution it is supposed to uphold.

The preceding discussion is an attempt to explain why medical decisions regarding handicapped infants are problematic, and why deciding who decides does not remove the problem. Some believe that, even if all *persons* have a right to life—and an equal right to have it protected—it does not follow that all *human beings* have those rights. They argue, and some courts have ruled, that human beings, that is, living members of the human species, have these and other rights, if, and only if, they are also "persons," and to be a person requires that a human being possess certain qualities. Thus, a noted Roman Catholic moral theologian, Richard McCormack, can write that *lives* are not equal, but *persons* are, and go on to say that "mere life" is not a value in itself,[14] but whether or not life is to be accepted as a value to be saved and to be saved equally depends upon a determination to be made by "a community of reasonable persons [as to] where the line is drawn and why."[15] When that determination is made, he alleges, we will be able to distinguish reasonable and unreasonable treatment, especially for those who cannot make the decisions for themselves. And, as McCormack suggests they should, people are hard at the task of drawing lines; but they are doing so in different ways and at different places.

Alan Donagan, a contemporary moral philosopher, noted recently that the abortion debate has spawned the argument that rights should be acquired or lost as human beings (or other beings) acquire or lose certain kinds of mental activity. Although some profess to have found some point of universal agreement on when a human attains and loses rights, differences abound. "But," Donagan remarks, "that is the nature of our contemporary concept of personhood: it is a do-it-yourself kit for constructing a 'moral community' to your own taste."[16]

The great diversity of conceptions of personhood precludes their full review in this essay. It must suffice to state that there is at least one important commitment shared by those who would draw a line between being a "human being" and being a "person." This line, however and wherever drawn, determines which members of the human species have rights and which do not. Furthermore, they agree that personhood, and having rights, are based on the ability to articulate desires and to choose the most rational means to achieve the desires articulated.

A much cited example of this way of defining personhood is that of Michael Tooley, who uses his definition to justify infanticide as well as abortion.[17] A "person," in Tooley's opinion, is an "organism" with a "serious right to life." Very carefully and precisely he identifies five states of being an organism must possess (or have possessed) in order to be said to have a serious right to life.[18] The stress is on an organism as having (or having had) a capacity to conceptualize and be conscious of itself as a continuous, experiencing subject of experiences and other mental states. Such an organism therefore must have (or must have had) a capacity to envisage a future for itself, and to have desires about its own future states. Why these powers or capacities? Because, having *rights* rests on having *desires,* and vio-

lations of rights are frustrations of those desires. This means that human fetuses (and any imaginable creature with only potential for a desire to live),
as well as newborn infants (and animals) who still lack such a desire have
no right to life. (Tooley leaves open the question as to whether certain
nonhuman organisms among animals have the desire and right to life: it is,
for him, a vexing, unresolved question.)

It is important to grasp the very special character of the "right to life"
and of "personhood" ascribed by Tooley. For example, a newborn kitten
has rights such as the right not to be tortured. A newborn kitten has this
right because a desire not to suffer pain can be ascribed to something that
lacks self-consciousness. Therefore, *rights* can be imputed to animals or
things by imputing *desires* to them. Then why cannot an infant be imputed
a desire to live? After all, rights, according to Tooley, are what self-conscious human beings desire, and doing what rational human beings want
or desire is the ultimate right.

This point becomes explicit when Tooley discusses any effort that might
be required of an individual if that individual is to honor someone's right
to life. Whether someone should exert great energy to save another individual's life will depend on something Tooley believes that the individual
who is in need of saving "has to take into account" before making the attempt, namely, *"his own right to do what he wants with his life."*[19] Presumably this is a right, as observed above, to ascribe rights to oneself and
others. Relative to a right to life, "persons" can require of others what
"persons" possess, namely a self-conscious desire to continue. Apparently,
then, "persons" have a right to choose death for newborns if and when
they desire death for them, and if and when they believe no self-conscious
desire for life can or should be ascribed to them as newborns.

Tooley and others see the power of the individual to articulate desires
self-consciously and rationally as a good in itself; and when this power is
gone, life, as a good, is questionable. As Marvin Kohl has stated it, the life
of an individual like Karen Ann Quinlan is meaningless. According to
Kohl, you cannot injure Karen Ann Quinlan by killing her. To kill her is
mercifully to end a mere existence that has none of the power we value as
calculating, choosing beings.[20]

Interestingly enough, Kohl rejects the notion of self-consciousness put
forward by Tooley, because Kohl perceives that we cannot know whether
Karen is self-conscious. Her helplessness, that is, her loss of the liberty
characteristic of rational agents, is what makes her life meaningless, and
makes her death a mercy to be desired by her and by people generally.

Englehardt, valuing this same liberty, sees children as having no inherent rights.[21] They are dependents lacking rational agency, and have only
the rights granted them. Again, rights are calculated, claimed, and ascribed
by those who have the power. He opposes killing children, but on the
purely practical ground that it might erode the necessary restraints on killing generally.

One argument against separating being a "human being" and being a "person" is that these definitions of personhood, although they vary as to "where the line is drawn," almost always relegate to the rank of a mere "human being" (with that rank's attendant exclusion of rights) more types of individuals than the definer intends or should intend.[22] Also the characteristics necessary to qualify as a "person" (with that rank's attendant right to life) are highly subjective; that is, they are often difficult to identify – or verify. Examples of the difficulty (impossibility?) of verification are cases such as Karen Ann Quinlan – or premature infants. Hence, it is highly probable that the constraint against killing generally will be applied arbitrarily. I find this argument persuasive, but those like Tooley remain unimpressed. For example, Tooley does not claim we can know when infants become persons (as he defines them); but that is no problem for him because the decisions he would make concerning the personhood of infants (for the purpose of determining their right to life) can be made soon after birth. Clearly, Tooley presumes that that most basic right – the liberty and power to *decide* rights – is a right possessed only by sufficiently developed rational agents – and infants do not qualify.

But, Tooley has left us with a number of puzzling and vexing questions. When are we rational enough to claim and ascribe as rights our own desires? And assuming I am rational enough, which desires am I morally obligated to cultivate and respect in others? This is especially critical because Tooley explicitly leaves open the question as to how much, in various instances, we would be obligated, or free, to pursue what we want with our lives even when that means failing to do something that would respect someone else's right to life. Tooley has left completely open, as morally unobjectionable, desires to kill, or to fail to save, oneself or others. Specifically, he has suggested that there will be times when our desire to kill an infant is justified. But he has not indicated what limits, if any, would be placed on these desires by moral considerations other than the decision as to whether a given infant can be said to have a desire to live. On what grounds does Tooley believe it is reasonable to expect agreement on ascribing such a desire to live; and what, in his view, does one do in the face of disagreement?

I suggest that there are certain moral constraints that have been, and should continue to be, recognized as such. Moreover, these moral constraints identify which desires and powers in human beings we are morally obligated to respect as human rights. Not every human desire is reasonably seen as morally acceptable and certainly there are human desires we are not obligated to foster or protect.

Imagine a recently escaped band of slaves (of any race) in the middle of a vast, scorching desert. Having been slaves, they have no voluntary organizations, no government, no enforcement agencies of any kind. Resources are scarce in a desert. People are prone to envy what others have, and to proceed from there to take things from them, seek sexual relations with the spouses of others, lie about who is doing any of these things, and when caught or frustrated, kill the ones who stand in the way of these envious desires to achieve lives of their own in accord with their own formulated wants.

What will become of this band of slaves if such inclinations are generally indulged? They will probably never make it through the desert alive; they will never thus become a people or a community with a land to live in together. They will perish as a group, and hence as individuals.

What can be done? The first consideration is that of identifying the locus of the power to live, and to live as a community. Such power is not in egoistic self-striving. Nor is it in governments, police forces, and armies. Hitler and others like him have sought that kind of power and it has utterly failed them. The possibility of community begins with acknowledging that the most powerful force in the universe is that force which has brought life into being and which is at the same time totally good, striving to deliver from oppression slaves and all others whose lives are held to be cheap, and who are exploited as means to others' ends. This force is life giving, freedom giving, and just. It moves to defend every human creature from being subordinated to others and their desires. Every human being is seen as a creature of this power.

Such an acknowledgment can be argued to be merely religious affirmation. Why should people so acknowledge? On the other hand, how can anyone acknowledge otherwise? Every individual who considers it rational to act one way or another *assumes* willy-nilly that it is possible to actualize the act or acts contemplated. If the power to actualize what is right or what is good is not present in humans, then every effort will be defeated. If one assumes that all our strivings will be ultimately defeated, or that even now evil is more powerful than good, why would it be rational to strive for human rights, or even definitions of personhood? As Camus has sagely observed, one believes in God in this sense, or the rational thing to do would be to commit suicide.

Furthermore, to be a community, as the Israelites and every other surviving group have seen, there must be constraints acknowledged and practiced against killing, stealing, lying, sexual infidelity, and envy. Again, this is a question of rationality. There are no rules, no laws, no order apart from the acceptance of these constraints. The rules of baseball can be rules only if they are not lies and are the same for everyone. Economic trade is precisely not stealing. If trade becomes stealing, violence or bondage follows.

Suppose you wished to go mountain climbing with someone. The night before you talk about human rights. Your companion tells you that rights are desires and desires are relative according to differing individual and community standards. What about killing, you timidly venture? That, says your associate, depends on the circumstances and what desires you wish to realize. Would you climb the mountain with such a person? I would not;

I value my life too much to do so. Surely, in a tough situation on the mountain I would become dispensable to such an individual.

There is another obligation acknowledged by various cultures: the honoring of one's father and mother. Here, procreation, that is, having a part in transmitting life and genetically endowed individuality, is something held in esteem. We have not chosen to be the self we are by heredity and through nurture. But, we can choose to continue community by transmitting and nurturing lives and selves. We can procreate, nurture, and educate lives. To do that requires the observation of all the constraints of the Decalogue against killing, lying, and the rest. Greek and Roman religions favoring abortion and infanticide were ultimately abandoned in favor of Judaism and Christianity.

Now we see where human rights come from. Human beings have rights within a community based on obligations that treat all human beings as *persons.* That is what Ramsey, and, hopefully, most of us are depending on. The task of reasonable human beings is to show that treating all humans as persons is rational and to do otherwise is not. It is to persuade people that human rights will be rationally and fairly respected only if, and only when, every human being is considered to be a person and entitled to be treated as such.

The question that remains, then, is whether one should ever have the right to kill one's self, or ascribe to others a "right" to be killed whether requested or not. In other words, to what extent should we sanction suicide, "mercy killing," and other death-producing actions, particularly when incompetents are the ones whose deaths are being contemplated?

Recently, Karen Lebacqz and H. Tristram Engelhardt have reviewed a series of traditional arguments against suicide and have found them wanting. They argue that "persons should be permitted to take their own lives when they have chosen to do so freely and rationally and when there are no other duties which would override this freedom."[23] However, they contend that suicide is usually wrong because it violates our "covenantal obligations to others," such as promise keeping, gratitude, reparation, and the like. Nevertheless, they believe there are three circumstances that justify suicide: (1) when it is impossible to discharge one's duties; (2) when suicide supports rather than violates obligations of covenant fidelity; and (3) when the intention of the suicide is to support the general good of persons and the conditions that make covenant fidelity possible.[24]

The first set of circumstances involves the issue of voluntary euthanasia. Lebacqz and Engelhardt argue that there are certain life circumstances, as in terminal illness accompanied by great pain, where it may be impossible to fulfill one's usual obligations. This being so, the right to suicide, which they claim is an extension of the general right to control over one's own body, is morally permissible.

This argument does not take into account the important alternatives that remain for the terminally ill. Dying persons retain the moral option of having their pain reduced. I argued earlier that it is morally justifiable to provide for a patient what may be the moral equivalent of a peaceful rest or vacation, such a provision not excluding the withdrawal of interventions that would prolong the process of dying. Relief of suffering that foreshortens the dying process does not require killing. As we noted above, it is possible to distinguish between shortening human life by killing and shortening human life by withholding medical interventions. One of the time-honored criteria in deciding whether killing can be morally justified is to ask whether it is a last resort. In the case of terminal illness, killing is not the only option and not the last resort.

The second circumstance justifying suicide is what Lebacqz and Engelhardt call covenant-affirming suicides: "suicide pacts" or self-sacrificial suicides where people would rather die than remain a burden to their families or to others. Here we see a rather narrow interpretation of the notion of "covenant" and "community." The fundamental basis of community is our agreement to live together in peaceful, nonviolent cooperation. We are all dependent on one another—and on one another's mercy. This is one reason why the injunction against killing is recognized as one of our most stringent obligations. An act of suicide, whatever agreements it might involve with some part of the community, is a violation of the covenant on which such communities are based. It is not strictly true to argue, as Lebacqz and Engelhardt do, that there are circumstances under which one no longer has any obligations to anyone. The obligations not to kill and not to engage in actions destructive of this principle remain to the very end of our lives. That is why it is important to bear in mind that the relief of pain does not require direct killing, and so does not require us to violate our obligation not to kill.

The third argument for suicide is what Lebacqz and Engelhardt call symbolic protest, or supporting the general good. Since they offer no specific illustrations, it is difficult to imagine what kinds of suicide Lebacqz and Engelhardt would wish to justify by this argument. Among our most revered and cherished saints, heroes, and heroines are those who have given their lives so that others might live. We do not, however, think of these actions as suicide. They represent circumstances where people place their lives in jeopardy for the sake of others. We can think of all kinds of instances, like smothering a hand grenade that is about to explode, stepping in front of an assailant's bullet, or being killed rather than reveal a secret so that others may live.

To justify dying under these circumstances, however, depends, as Lebacqz and Engelhardt rightly discern, upon what our act symbolizes. Killing oneself symbolizes a direct repudiation of the general injunction against killing and of the covenant on which our communities are based. If, however, we willfully choose not to avoid certain death for the sake of saving another person's life, such a choice symbolizes the same high value placed on human life that the constraint against killing is designed to foster. Where "symbolic protest" involves virtual certainty that death may result from the action in question, or a high risk of death, it may be morally justified if it symbolizes the affirmation of life.

Consider the doubtless well-intentioned individuals who burned themselves to death protesting the war in Vietnam as an example of what Lebacqz and Engelhardt may wish to condone. For Americans in particular, this action was certainly not a last resort. I see no reason why these same individuals could not have made their symbolic protest by entering villages under bombardment and using their bodies, for example, to smother the flames from the clothes of napalmed children. The difference between this way of dying, or risking death, as against simply burning oneself, is that throwing oneself on the body of a burning child precisely honors the distinction between *taking* one's life and *giving* one's life, and entails the actual and symbolic hope that thereby some lives now—and lives in the future—may possibly be saved.

Ultimately, each of us has an obligation to encourage respect for the preciousness of life, the fostering of which has made our own lives possible until our dying day. The only circumstances under which we could feel confident that it is right to give or yield our lives would be those in which we have a clear opportunity through our death to save, affirm, and protect life. People who are dying are not expected to be heroic either by extending their lives or by giving it up for others. What we do expect is that they refrain from acts that diminish rather than enhance the value we place on life. On this view, we would not ascribe to incompetent human beings a right to be killed, whatever desires we may speculate they have. Nor would inability to find in them a desire to live lead us to give up our usual constraints against killing fellow humans.

The choice to live and to refrain from killing is one of the foundations of any community—and of its prospects for continuation. Moses, addressing the people of Israel near the end of his life, made this point so very long ago.

> I have set before you life and death, blessing and curse; therefore choose life, that you and your descendants may live.[25]

Notes

1. P. RAMSEY, ETHICS AT THE EDGES OF LIFE 317 (1978).

2. Rachels, *Active and Passive Euthanasia*, 292 NEW ENGLAND J. MED. 78 (1975).

3. *Id.* at 79.

4. Saunders, *The Case of the Dying Patient and His Family*, 1972 CONTACT 38 (Supp. Summer 1972).

5. Duff & Campbell, *Moral and Ethical Dilemmas in the Special-Care Nursery,* 289 NEW ENGLAND J. MED. 890 (1973).

6. Inglefinger, *Bedside Ethics for the Hopeless Case,* 289 NEW ENGLAND J. MED. 914 (1973).

7. Lorber, *Results of Treatment of Myelomeningocele: An Analysis of 524 Unselected Cases with Special Reference to Possible Selection for Treatment,* 13 DEVELOPMENTAL MED. CHILD NEUROLOGY SUPPLEMENT 279 (1971).

8. Freedman, *To Treat or Not to Treat: Ethical Dilemmas of Treating the Infant with a Myelomeningocele,* 20 CLINICAL NEUROSURGERY 134 (1972).

9. *See, e.g.,* cases cited in Robertson, *Involuntary Euthanasia of Defective Newborns: A Legal Analysis,* 27 STAN. L. REV. 213 (1973).

10. *In re* Quinlan, 70 N.J. 10, 355 A.2d 647 (1976).

11. Superintendent of Belchertown v. Saikewicz, 370 N.E.2d 417 (1977).

12. Under *Roe v. Wade,* the human fetus is not afforded legal status as a person. Roe v. Wade, 410 U.S. 113 (1973).

13. Levine v. Institutions & Agencies Dep't of New Jersey, 84 N.J. 234, 418 A.2d 229 (1980).

14. McCormick, *The Quality of Life, the Sanctity of Life,* 8 HASTINGS CENTER REP. 30 (1978).

15. *Id.* at 36.

16. A. DONAGAN, THE THEORY OF MORALITY 170 (1977). Donagan believes, and I agree, that there is a decisive, objective ground for questioning the efforts to separate being human and being a person.

> Duties owed to any being arise out of the respect that is owed to it. Let it, then be provisionally conceded that, in the first instance, respect is recognized as owed to beings by virtue of a state they are in: say, that of rational agency. If there are beings who reach that state by a process of development natural to normal members of their species, given normal nurture, must not respect logically be accorded to them, whether they have yet reached that state or not? The principle underlying this reasoning is: if respect is owed to beings because they are in a certain state, it is owed to whatever, by its very nature, develops into that state. To reject this principle would be arbitrary, if indeed it would be intelligible. What could be made of somebody who professed to rate the state of rational agency as of supreme value, but who regarded as expendable any rational creature whose powers were as yet undeveloped?
> Since it would be arbitrary to accord the respect that generates moral duties to beings in a state of developed rationality, while refusing it to beings who naturally develop into that state, there is a fundamental moral difference between a member of the species homo sapiens, or of any other species of rational animal there may be in the universe, and a cat or a sparrow. "Ye are of more value than many sparrows" even when your natural development is at the foetal stage.

17. Tooley, *A Defense of Abortion and Infanticide,* in PROBLEMS OF ABORTION 51 (J. Feinberg ed. 1973).

18. *Id.* at 54–60.

19. *Id.* at 85.

20. Kohl, *Karen Quinlan: Human Rights and Wrongful Killing,* in BIOETHICS AND HUMAN RIGHTS 121 (E. Bandman & B. Bandman eds. 1978)

21. Engelhardt, *Ethical Issues in Aiding the Death of Young Children,* in BENEFICIENT EUTHANASIA 180 (M. Kohl ed. 1975).

22. *See, e.g.,* the carefully argued article, Sherlock, *Selective Non-Treatment of Newborns: A Critique,* 7 ETHICS IN SCI. & MED. 111 (1980).

23. Lebacqz & Engelhardt, *Suicide,* in DEATH, DYING AND EUTHANASIA 689 (D. Horan & D. Mall eds. 1977).

24. Ibid.

25. *Deuteronomy* 30:15-19 (Revised Standard).

Index